DYE: a memoir of art, music, faith, family and hair color

DYE

a memoir
of art, music,
faith, family
and hair color

BRAD JOHNS

with

MARIANNE DOUGHERTY

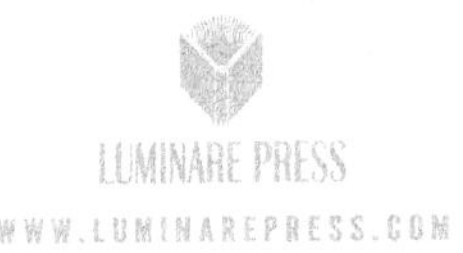

LUMINARE PRESS
WWW.LUMINAREPRESS.COM

DYE
a memoir of art, music, faith, fashion and hair color
Copyright © 2023 by Brad Johns with Marianne Dougherty

Printed in the United States of America

Luminare Press
442 Charnelton St.
Eugene, OR 97401
www.luminarepress.com

LCCN: 2023913528
ISBN: 979-8-88679-185-3

For Shari, my North Star,
and for Grace, Thelma and Alice,
my Sacred Feminine

Do you not see how necessary a
world of pains and troubles is to school
an intelligence and make it a soul?

—JOHN KEATS

PROLOGUE

Even now I can see it all so clearly: New York City when disco is the only music that matters. The syncopated baselines. The soaring string sections. The horns. The whole thing peaks in 1977 with John Travolta and that fucking white suit. Now straight, middle-class white kids are pouring in from the suburbs to wait in line at Studio 54 or Xenon. Studio 54 is nothing but fashion bullshit anyway. If Bianca Jagger is there, you know that Halston dressed her.

But downtown? Downtown is a whole other story, and it belongs to us: the gay, Black or Latino kids who go to Club Mars or Infinity or the Paradise Garage, which is literally a garage in the West Village. A dance floor big enough to accommodate 2,000 people with a Black DJ named Larry Levan spinning records all night. Larry Levan invented house music. Larry Levan is a genius.

The Garage has the best sound system in the city and a sprung dance floor that has just the right amount of give so you feel like you're bouncing. Bouncing to Larry Levan's remix of "Ain't No Mountain High Enough" by Inner Life. Or the 12" club version of "Heartbeat" by Taana Gardner: *Heartbeat, it makes me feel so weak.*

You have to be a member to belong to the "Gay-rage." They give you a piece of metal shaped like a wrench; it looks like one of those things you'd find in a child's toolbox. If you don't have that key, you don't get in. Keith Haring and Robert Mapplethorpe are members. You see them waiting in line just like everyone else.

Robert Mapplethorpe is breathtaking, but I've never had the courage to approach him even though we have something in common. He and Patti Smith were boyfriend and girlfriend for a few years just like me and Viv, a girl I met in acting class who's my best friend in the whole world. When I came to New York, we were boyfriend and girlfriend too until I decided that I liked boys better.

Viv is worried about me. She thinks my drug use is spiraling out of control. Maybe she's right. I had to go to the dentist for something, a filling maybe, and he told me that if I don't stop doing speed all my teeth are going to fall out.

The thing is, I need to take a carefully orchestrated combination of pharmaceuticals to function: six to nine Black Beauties to keep me focused at work and four to six Tuinals at night to keep from crashing. Without those drugs I'd be curled up on the sofa listening to Laura Nyro and thinking about suicide.

Blue is my favorite color. When I was a little kid, I made taffy with my grandmother, but it had to be blue taffy. My first car was a blue Rambler that my father got for $200. A powerful combination of two barbiturates, Tuinal comes in bullet-shaped capsules: red on one end, blue on the other, which might be part of its allure. It also carries a high risk of overdose. Maybe that's why Viv is so worried about me.

A group of us goes out dancing almost every night: me and Viv, my friend Chris, a couple of my gay friends and a girl we know named Amber, who has a Black pimp and turns tricks at a fancy apartment building uptown for

    Brad Johns with Marianne Dougherty

extra cash. In the Deuce you can get a blowjob for $25, but Amber works out of a high-rise on 51st Street where prices start at $250 and go up from there depending on what you want. Amber says that the girls never get busted because they give free blowjobs to the cops who look the other way.

We check in with each other before going out so we don't end up wearing the same thing. I'm finally slim enough to fit into women's Wranglers with a 26-inch waist, a tiny T-shirt and leather boots with six-inch heels that I push down around my ankles. They hurt like hell, but that's the price you pay if you want to look good.

One night we show up at the Roxy in varying shades of blue, yellow, purple and white. We look like a bouquet. Or a flock of rare exotic birds. The girls aren't wearing underwear so people will gasp when they twirl around on the dance floor and their skirts fly up, offering a glimpse of pubic hair clipped to resemble a daisy or a triangle. We look so fabulous that the guy manning the door calls out, "Brad and his crew!" and waves us into the club.

There's a bar on Second Avenue called the Sahara. Lipstick lesbians dressed like models. Lesbians in jackets and ties. They love us gays though so I stop in from time to time. When "Love Hangover" by Diana Ross comes on, every fag and lesbian in the place hits the dance floor. One night I see a girl there I used to go out with.

"You gay now?" I ask her.

She raises one eyebrow. "Are you?"

"Yeah," I shout over the music and we both laugh.

Of all the gay clubs in New York, Infinity is my favorite. It's as long as a football field with a set of bleachers on one end where you can sit in the dark and do a line of coke. There's always a crowd of people from New Jersey and Connecticut. We're like rival gangs, but they all know that we Manhattan queens run the show.

We like to get our dance on at Infinity before we go our separate ways. Chris usually splits for the Garage. I prefer 12 West, a members-only club that doesn't serve alcohol, which is why it can stay open all night. A lot of closeted gay actors go there. A former flower factory, it has ten mirror balls suspended above the dance floor, bowls of punch spiked with LSD and a sound system that rivals the Garage.

One night Viv and I take a cab to The Spike, a classic S&M bar on Eleventh Avenue by the West Side Highway. Ultra-butch veneer. Every surface is painted black. The DJ is a Black guy with a shaved head who plays mostly rock, no disco, but no one's dancing anyway.

When Viv decides to go home early, I head over to an after-hours sex club on 14th Street called The Anvil. The bouncers are as sleazy as the bar itself, and they all look like body builders. Felipe Ross is on the bar in full Indian headdress when I walk in. You know, the guy from the Village People. They dance on the bar here all the time. We all whoop it up when they do "Y.M.C.A." because we know what goes on at the Young Men's Christian Association on 57th Street. It's no secret that guys come in from Jersey or Long Island to get a room and hook up with someone for the weekend. It makes me laugh when I hear that straight people in the suburbs are dancing to this song at weddings.

So, a guy in full leather walks up to me and says, "I want to take you home with me." He's a foot taller than I am, probably about 6'6" or so with sandy brown hair. I feel like I've been singled out. Like I've just won gay bingo and am going home with a toaster oven. We go outside where his motorcycle is parked at the curb. I've never been on a

    Brad Johns with Marianne Dougherty

motorcycle before, and I hang on for dear life while we zig and zag up Ninth Avenue to his apartment.

I pop a Tuinal and offer one to him, which he accepts.

"So, what are we going to do?" I ask while he's undressing me.

"I'm going to tie you up." He picks up a length of rope like one a cowboy would use to lasso a horse. Then he trusses me up like a chicken.

I'm still not sure what's about to happen, but there's a thick metal hook hanging from the ceiling. He's a big guy, and he lifts me over his head and hangs me from that hook like a sack of dirty laundry.

"Now I'm going to fuck you," he tells me right before he passes out.

"Hey, wake up," I shout, but he's out like a light. From my vantage point, I can tell that he just pissed the bed. I wriggle around trying to free myself, but it's no use. It must be five in the morning, and all I can think about is that I have a 10 a.m. facial that I'm probably going to miss.

A few months later Viv and I are at Infinity. It's freezing outside so I'm wearing the black leather jumpsuit I got at T. Jones on Park Avenue and a pair of seven-inch platform shoes from Jumping Jack Flash. I'm pretty high, but something's not right. Now my hands are twitching. After I do a face-plant on the dance floor where I'm thrashing around like a fish out of water or someone having a seizure, the thought occurs to me that I might be dying.

At first no one seems to notice what's happening. Gloria Gaynor blares from the speakers. Now someone is grabbing me by the ankles while someone else nearly yanks my arms out of their sockets. I am carried outside where I'm literally thrown into the gutter by two beefy bouncers, who shake their heads as they walk back inside. Someone is screaming. Who? Vivian? The cries become more frantic. *Help us! Help us!*

A cab screeches to a halt near the curb, and Vivian throws a wad of cash at the driver. *Help me. Please.*

Viv gives the cabbie our address. She knows better than to take me to the hospital. I have big plans for my life, and I can't have a record.

One of my platform shoes is missing. One hundred bucks down the drain. Drifting in and out of consciousness, I'm seventeen again staring at a pair of powder-blue platform shoes in the window of Thom McAn in downtown Pittsburgh. If I could just have those shoes, I thought, I could do anything. Somehow my mother came up with the money, and I wore those shoes to my audition at the Stella Adler School of Acting in New York City.

Like Dorothy's ruby slippers, I believed those shoes had the power to transport me anywhere I wanted to go. Now I am exactly where I wanted to be, but nothing has turned out like I expected. What happened to me, I wonder. Then I black out.

  Brad Johns with Marianne Dougherty

— **1** —

Like every story, mine begins the day my parents met at a nightclub in McKees Rocks, a suburb of Pittsburgh. A gifted trumpet player, Phillip Carlton Johns was the only white member of a progressive jazz band that was performing that night, but he had played in backup bands all over the country for some of the greats like Billie Holliday and Dizzy Gillespie. There's something inherently sexy about trumpet players. Think of Miles Davis, Chet Baker. Maybe that's what drew my mother to my father in the first place.

With her Italian-Yugoslavian roots, Thelma Rose Ciccone resembled Linda Darnell, the "girl with the perfect face" according to those in the know in Hollywood. With his French-English ancestry, my father must have seemed as exotic to her as she did to him. My mother loved jazz almost as much as my father did, and as she sat at the bar nursing a highball and listening to the music, my father made the decision to cross the room and introduce himself as soon as the band took a break. Their attraction was immediate and palpable, and on the last day of June, 1951, Thelma Rose Ciccone became Thelma Rose Johns.

The newlyweds moved into a beautiful two-bedroom apartment, and on weekends they went to upscale nightclubs in downtown Pittsburgh like Lenny Litman's Copa that offered three shows a night and booked acts like Ella

Fitzgerald and Miles Davis. Occasionally they'd take my mother's younger sister Alice along.

I have a photograph of the three of them with a group of family and friends that was probably taken by the Copa's house photographer. My father had studied tailoring, and he is wearing a baby-blue suit he made himself to match the color of his eyes. One leg crossed casually over the other, he looks directly into the camera, confident and self-assured, but it's hard to tell what he's thinking. Alice is on his left in a dress of taffeta or maybe silk shantung, one hand beneath her chin, dark lipstick that matches her nail color (Revlon's Cherries in the Snow), hair fashionably coiffed. My mother, in a halter-top dress, arms crossed at the waist, simply looks bored. A straw pokes out of her mixed drink, probably a whiskey sour, her favorite. Years later my father would describe my mother as a malcontent.

When I was born four years into their marriage, my father quit playing the trumpet, simply "put it down." The life of an itinerant musician, he reasoned—always on the road, playing a different club in a different city each night— was no kind of life for a man with a family. So, he took a manufacturing job, a decision that shifted the dynamic between my parents. My mother felt that she had married a jazz musician with unlimited prospects. Now he'd given it all up and for what? A dead-end job in a factory? That wasn't the life she'd signed up for, and she let him know it.

Things can always get worse, of course, and they did when my father lost the sight in one eye (a tumor was misdiagnosed) and was fired from his factory job. Moving into a housing project called Ohio View Acres when I was four was a fall from grace, and it changed everything.

     Brad Johns with Marianne Dougherty

Built in 1942 as temporary housing for war workers manufacturing Landing Ship Tanks or LSTs on Neville Island in McKees Rocks, OVA had become dilapidated and rundown, a series of dun-colored clapboard row houses with patchy front lawns. Most of the war workers had decamped to fashionable ranch houses or two-story Colonials in newer neighborhoods with better school districts, and our neighbors were either on welfare or just down on their luck.

We were officially poor now, and the life my parents had built together where music was the common denominator slowly unraveled. There were no more nights dining and dancing at one of the swanky nightclubs in the city. Boxing up the records they'd played on the stereo in that beautiful two-bedroom apartment, the music simply stopped for both of them, and for me.

Denied the life she had imagined, Thelma Rose Johns felt cheated. I loved my mother, but if you crossed her, she'd freeze you out, and that's what she did to my father.

It was brutal growing up in a house with parents who were at war with one another. My mother could be cruel, calling my father a "one-eyed failure" and worse. It must have been difficult for him to take her abuse because he was, at heart, a gentle soul. He and his sister had been placed in an orphanage when they ran away from home to escape their abusive father, and he told me that he hated it when "they made me get in the ring and box."

When my brother Craig was born in 1959, I understood very quickly that my parents were either unwilling or unable to take care of him, or me for that matter. I seem to have no recollection of my parents being around when Craig and I were little. So, where were they? My mother could have been playing cards with some of the women in the neighborhood like she often did. My father might have been at the junkyard looking for parts he could use to repair one of our cars, a series of clunkers that were always breaking down. I honestly don't know.

One afternoon when I crept into my parents' bedroom to check on Craig, who was asleep in his crib, I saw a spider crawling up his blanket toward his face. Instinctively I killed it.

That's when I heard a voice just over my right shoulder: *You must take care of your family from now on, but I'll be there to guide you. Will you take on this job?*

Was God asking me to protect my baby brother from harm? I sensed that He might be, and because I loved my brother and my parents, I was more than willing to accept the responsibility. No five-year-old child should be made to carry that kind of burden, but I did, and I carried it well into adulthood.

When Craig was just a year old my mother found herself pregnant again, and she was not happy about it. She had already made it very clear to me that she did not love my father anymore, and I suspected that it would fall to me, again, to be the adult. The only difference was that now I'd have two siblings who would require my protection.

The day my sister was born, my father took me to the hospital where my mother leaned out the window and asked me what she should name the baby.

"Call her Shari," I shouted because I loved Shari Lewis, who appeared on *Captain Kangaroo* with her sock puppet, Lamb Chop.

What can I say about Shari except that she is my North Star, the one person I have always been able to depend on, and I would do anything for her. When she was born, all

     Brad Johns with Marianne Dougherty

I wanted to do was make things right in my family, and I knew that I'd have to start by making my mother happy. So, I became her helper, cleaning house, washing the dishes, picking out drapes for the living room (even then I had an eye for color), using my little calculator to keep a running tab when we went to the grocery store to avoid the embarrassment of having to put things back when she didn't have enough money to pay for all of the items in our cart.

Unlike her sister, who was slender, my mother struggled with her weight. To curb her appetite, a doctor prescribed Eskatrol, a popular amphetamine doled out like candy until 1981. I noticed that the pills made her happy, so it's not surprising that years later amphetamines became my drug of choice to deal with isolation and sadness. The downside was how unhappy she became after she crashed. That's how speed works. It's like borrowing tomorrow's energy and using it today.

When my mother invited her friends over to play pinochle, Craig and I acted like her little butlers, refilling everyone's drinks and refreshing the chip bowls. Everyone was high on speed so there was lots of high-pitched laughter as they played cards until well past midnight. Then, when the pills started to wear off, the energy in the room seemed to shift. The women all had sour looks on their faces now, and there was a litany of complaints. One of them might announce that she was going to throw her husband, that SOB, out when she got home. As the mood became increasingly dark, I'd take Craig aside.

"It's time for us to go upstairs," I'd whisper, and we'd tiptoe out of the room.

My mother and I were inseparable when I was growing up, but ours was a dysfunctional relationship: a classic case of transference. She simply redirected the feelings she may have had for my father at one time to me.

I couldn't have been much older than six or seven when I asked her, "Am I your husband now?" and she answered, without hesitation, "Yes."

I have lived my adult life as a gay man, but in high school I went out with girls, which did not sit well with my mother, who wanted me all to herself. In college at New York University, I was attracted to both men and women, but instinctively I knew that my mother would not allow herself to be replaced.

On the occasions I'd bring a girl home, my mother would take me into the kitchen and narrow her eyes. Her assessment was always the same: "She's a whore."

It was different when I came home with a guy. Her face lit up when he walked into the room where she invited him to sit next to her.

"What do you do for a living," she asked one of my dates. "Oh, you work for the airlines? Are you a flight attendant?"

"No, I'm a cargo agent," he said, which seemed to suit her just fine.

Each time she peppered my date with questions—*Where are your parents from? Do you go to church? Do you have any brothers or sisters?*—it became clear that she was conducting an interview to determine if this one was good enough for her. Not me. Her.

Would I have made different choices if I'd had a different kind of mother? It's hard to know. What I have come to realize is that I didn't make that choice; that choice was made for me.

     Brad Johns with Marianne Dougherty

2

had never seen the ocean, had never been anywhere really, when my aunt Alice took me to Wildwood. She and her two children, my cousins Lynn and Chris, were living with my grandparents on McCoy Road in McKees Rocks. Each morning, Alice took the bus downtown to Mellon Bank where she worked as a secretary. I doubt she made that much money, yet she managed to save enough to take Lynn and Chris to the Jersey Shore every year. One summer—I must have been about thirteen years old—she asked me if I wanted to come along.

Wildwood is located on a barrier island facing the Atlantic Ocean on the southernmost tip of New Jersey. To the north are Ocean City and Atlantic City, Long Beach Island and Asbury Park. Wildwood had been a party town since the 1950s. Bill Haley & His Comets performed "Rock Around the Clock" at the HofBrau Hotel in Wildwood on Memorial Day weekend, 1954. Chubby Checker introduced "The Twist" at the Rainbow Club, and *American Bandstand* broadcast live on occasion from the Starlight Ballroom.

I'm not sure I ever told my aunt how much her generosity meant to me, but I hope she knew. I can't imagine that she owned an automobile, so she may have borrowed my grandfather's black Cadillac, a boat of a car (used, of course) with outrageous tail fins. We took the Pennsylvania Turnpike, stopping for lunch at Howard Johnson's, a restaurant I had never visited because my mother said that we couldn't afford to eat there. We sat in a booth with a Formica table and ordered from laminated menus. I have no recollection of what I ate, but I remember the feeling I had, like waking up in Oz, a technicolor world of aqua and orange.

The midcentury modern motels with space-age architecture and kidney-shaped swimming pools that were springing up all over town were too expensive, so we stayed in one of the guest houses that were popular then: stately Victorian homes that had been single-family residences before they were sold and subdivided. The formal living room on the first floor was a kind of welcome center where you checked in and picked up the key to your room. Upstairs were multiple bedrooms, some with a shared bath down the hall. Alice had her own room, while Lynn, Chris and I bunked together. I was fascinated by the pressed glass doorknobs, which were clearly from another era and unlike anything I had ever seen in OVA.

Famous for its seven-mile stretch of wide sandy beaches (free of charge, which was rare), Wildwood had a world-class boardwalk with dozens of small shops jammed with merchandise like T-shirts, costume jewelry, beach balls and pails. There were restaurants like Grandma's (a likeness of her face next to the flashing neon sign beamed down as you passed by) or the French-themed Pierre's (out of our price range) with a mural of Paris on the wall and accordion music playing in the background. Laura's Fudge also had salt water taffy, and pizza places like Macks sold huge pies dripping with oil and gooey with cheese. Air-conditioned movie theaters showed the latest releases, and you could play miniature golf or ride the roller coaster or Ferris wheel on the amusement pier. In Pittsburgh we had Kennywood

     Brad Johns with Marianne Dougherty

Park with world-class wooden rollercoasters like the Thunderbolt and the Jack Rabbit so we didn't waste what little money we had on rides, but we walked that boardwalk every night.

Alice tanned easily and looked like an Italian film star in just a couple of days. Dressed in capri pants and orange flats to match her lipstick, she took us to buy ice cream (my favorite flavor was pistachio) and allowed me to buy a string of love beads, which all the hippies were wearing to signify peace and love. I never took them off except to go into the ocean.

In the morning, lifeguards raised the American flag before climbing onto their wooden towers, applying zinc oxide to their noses so they wouldn't burn and holding court for the teenage girls who dropped by to flirt. I liked to get to the beach early each morning to find a good spot, unfurling one of the blankets we brought from home and digging a pair of cheap round sunglasses with pink lenses out of my bag.

One afternoon I saw a couple lying on a blanket not far from ours. He had wavy hair to his waist; hers was long too, but straight. *Hippies?* They were lying on their stomachs, and I watched while he casually placed one hand, lovingly it seemed to me, on her hip. I had never seen my parents or anyone else I knew display that kind of affection, and it made a big impression on me.

Sensing my confusion, Alice explained that they were "in love." Apparently, that's what love looked like; I had just never seen it before.

I looked for that couple every day after that the way a birdwatcher might scan the horizon hoping to spot some rare, exotic species: a red-crowned crane or a Honduran

Emerald. One night I caught a glimpse of them walking barefoot in bell-bottom jeans on the boardwalk. *Could I find someone to love me like that someday*, I wondered.

The best part about that vacation? *They* weren't there. It was peaceful and quiet. Alice never lost her temper; there was no shouting and screaming. Even that couple on the beach had radiated stillness. They seemed in sync, in harmony, a team, and I wanted what they had. It would take years for me to experience that kind of love, but just seeing that it was possible gave me hope.

That trip to Wildwood was a turning point because it introduced me to a wider world outside of OVA, outside of Pittsburgh. Growing up, there were other seminal moments as well. When I was nine or ten, I became infatuated with three sisters who lived in our neighborhood. Bertha, the oldest, dyed her hair a rich shade of chestnut. The middle sister, Roberta (everyone called her Sparky because she had a temper) wore white lipstick and nail polish to match her typing-paper white hair, which she wore in a bouffant with spit curls on the side. Arlene, the youngest (we called her Leni) had a pixie cut the color of honey. With a pound of foundation on their faces, two sets of false eyelashes and flawlessly executed cat-eye makeup, they seemed incredibly modern and sexy. In the summer, they wore pants hemmed at mid-calf called clam diggers, midriff-baring angel tops and pointy-toed sling-back flats. Looking up at them in their bullet bras, all I saw was an "M" beneath those Maybelline faces.

They were our babysitters on the rare occasions that our parents went out for the evening, and that's when the fun started. Bertha, Sparky and Leni were our Shangri-Las, one of the few girl groups who were white, not Black. They

    Brad Johns with Marianne Dougherty

taught us how to do The Swim, The Pony and The Hitch-Hike, and we'd wave our stuck-out thumbs and dance with wild abandon, even Shari, who was only about four or five years old. We had a record player, and we'd reverently slip our 45s out of their protective sleeves to keep from scratching them, place them on the turntable and sing along to "Soldier Boy" by The Shirelles and "He's So Fine" by The Chiffons.

Music has sustained me through good times and bad, and I can thank those teenage girls for introducing me to music that became the soundtrack of my life growing up. I'd discover Led Zeppelin while in high school, and later rap and hip-hop, but it was those girl groups of the '60s that taught me about relationships: sometimes you have to wait for the right person to come along ("You Can't Hurry Love" by The Supremes); sometimes a night of passion alters someone's feelings about us ("Will You Love Me Tomorrow" by The Shirelles); sometimes we love the wrong person ("Leader of the Pack" by The Shangri-Las); sometimes love turns violent ("He Hit Me and It Felt Like a Kiss" by The Crystals). When I had sex for the first time, it was Barbara Mason's "Yes, I'm Ready" that played on a loop in my head.

If I was destined to become a world-class colorist, the seeds may have been planted in OVA. Bertha, Sparky and Leni, who were certainly not going to go through life in the hair color God gave them, were muses. One of our neighbors dyed her hair green every St. Patrick's Day, and my aunt Alice used henna once a week to add a "tinge of auburn" to her hair. All of my mother's friends wanted to be blondes, and who could blame them? After all, blondes have more fun. Or at least that's what those ads for Miss Clairol suggested. When Shirley Polykoff, who wrote that ad, was asked if she believed those words, she responded, "There's power in being a blonde, it's a way of life." She had a point.

Who knew that years later I'd become famous for my "buttery blondes" or that I'd be the Global Color Director for Clairol? Life is unpredictable that way.

When you grow up like I did, it's hard to imagine a different life for yourself. There was a luxury apartment building in downtown Pittsburgh called Gateway Towers, and when I asked my mother what kind of people lived there, she said, "rich people."

The implication, of course, was that people like us had no hope of living in a place like that, but I think I had already decided that I'd be the kind of person who would live in a place like that. My dream came true when I finally made enough money to afford a studio apartment in that iconic building to use as a crash pad when I visited my family. By then, I owned my apartment on Perry Street in the West Village and had paid for the house in Bellevue, a suburb of Pittsburgh across the river from OVA, where my parents and siblings lived.

When Clairol offered me an exorbitant sum of money for my expertise, I paid cash for a beachfront property of my own in Long Beach, New York, about three hours away from Wildwood where I'd spent that idyllic summer vacation so long ago. I called it the "sandcastle Clairol built."

3

My grandmother's house was a safe haven for me and my siblings when we were growing up, and Saturday nights were special because we spent them with her. Sometimes she'd go to the local bar for fish sandwiches so big we could barely wrap our hands around them. Then, after dinner, she'd pull out an old cookbook and we'd make something sweet like fudge. One weekend I asked her if we could make taffy, and she flipped through the pages of her cookbook until she found a recipe for it.

Because my favorite color was blue, I asked if we could make blue taffy.

She grew thoughtful, considering my request. "You know that taffy is usually red," she told me, and my heart fell. Then her face lit up. "Okay, let's do it!"

I loved her for giving me permission to break the rules that way, to make blue taffy instead of red, and I'm certain that she gave me the confidence to do the same thing when I became a colorist.

In the summer when she called our house to say, "They're ready," we knew she meant the blackberries. Dressed in long-sleeved shirts, Shari, Craig and I would head into a patch of land behind OVA that had been a farmer's field to pick blackberries until our hands bled from the sharp thorns. Then we'd head home carrying bowls of plump, inky-black fruit that my grandmother would transform into turnovers or pies. Turnovers were my favorite because you could pick them up and eat them out of your hand like Pop-Tarts, only better.

First, she'd make the filling, tossing the berries with sugar and cornstarch. If she needed more blackberries, we'd dash back into the field. Then, the kitchen fragrant with the aroma of fruit and sugar, she'd start on the crust, combining flour, salt and cold water in a bowl and using two forks to cut in the lard before transferring the dough to a floured work surface. After dusting her own hands with flour, she'd fold the dough into a ball and roll it out before placing it into a pie pan. Once the crust was filled, she'd arrange strips of dough in a basketweave pattern on top and sprinkle a bit of sugar on each one for a crunchy, caramelized sweetness. Then we'd be dispatched to the living room to wait for the pies to bake, which seemed to take forever. When we were called back into the kitchen, every available surface—the table, the countertops—was filled with pies.

One thing I have never forgotten about my grandmother's house is how the walls in her living room were crowded with my uncle Kenny's paintings: interiors, self-portraits, scenes from ancient Rome, a perfect likeness of John F. Kennedy, the first Catholic president. Kenny graduated from the Art Institute of Pittsburgh, but he never did anything with his degree because my grandfather told him the arts were full of "queers."

After a tour of duty in Korea where he was in combat, Kenny moved in with my grandparents and drank all day long, often passing out in a chair where he had nightmares about being in a foxhole with rats crawling all over him. Sensitive and socially awkward, he seemed angry all the time, and there were rumors that he beat his girlfriends. He also had a secret that he kept from all of us for years, but we knew nothing about any of that when we were children and my grandmother's house seemed like a respite from daily life in the projects.

Reading offered the same kind of escape for me well into high school. I had been bullied for as long as I could remember, but if I stayed on the porch all summer with a book, my tormentors couldn't bother me.

Once a week, my father drove me to the public library where I was permitted to take out six books at a time. I was a voracious reader who tore through all of the classics that were on a list one of my teachers had given me: *Forever Amber, Les Miserables, Tale of Two Cities, Wuthering Heights.* My favorite was *Jane Eyre,* which I read four times, but I also read popular fiction like *Gone With the Wind* and *Rosemary's Baby.* One of my favorite non-fiction books was *The Strawberry Statement,* which was about the takeover of the office of the dean of Columbia University by student protestors.

My mother and my aunt Alice had no discernable domestic skills. It was my grandmother who kept house, and she took it seriously: cleaning the kitchen on Monday, vacuuming on Tuesday, doing the laundry on Wednesday and so on. Watching her put a meal together gave me the skills required to see dozens of clients each day. My grandmother could have four burners going at one time, while she was also peeling potatoes, chopping vegetables or doing any number of other tasks that enabled her to put dinner on the table. Later, in the salon, I juggled eight clients at a time, moving seamlessly between the chairs to lift the foils and check the progress of someone's highlights or apply a glaze to a double-processed blonde.

Like hair color, cooking is chemistry. Peroxide acts as an oxidizing agent when mixed with hair dye, which is how you lift color. Cook an onion slowly over heat and the natural sugar (sucrose) will be transformed to a simple form of sugar that tastes sweeter. So, remember, the next time you enjoy an omelet with caramelized onions, you have science to thank.

Watching my grandmother in her kitchen also taught me about the importance of timing, which is critical if you're a colorist. Leave a pot of stew on the stove too long and it burns. Leave color on a client's hair too long and it turns to mush. I learned that from her.

Like all of the women in my family, my grandmother was complicated. Her parents disowned her when she became pregnant at fifteen, and when she delivered my mother on the kitchen table, my grandfather was nowhere to be found. Presumably he was with one of the women he kept on the side. Years later my grandmother opened up about the abuse she endured as a young wife when my grandfather used to beat her, kicking her so hard in the stomach on two occasions that she miscarried.

Abuse is passed down in families, like brown eyes or freckles, and my grandmother took her anger and frustration out on my mother, who in turn took her anger and frustration out on my sister. Still, she was my rock, and those afternoons in her kitchen were magical.

4

Music has always played an important role in my life. My parents bonded over their love of jazz so maybe it's in my DNA. All I know is that I would never have survived adolescence if it wasn't for Laura Nyro, who wrote a lot of songs that became number-one hits for other artists. The 5th Dimension covered "Wedding Bell Blues" and "Stone Soul Picnic," while Barbra Streisand recorded "Stoney End."

I discovered Laura Nyro purely by accident. When we lived in the projects, we did our grocery shopping at Kroger, which also sold 45 rpm records in sealed plastic bags. Records that found their way into those grab bags might not have sold well in stores, or maybe they were defective in some way. You never knew what you were getting until you took them home, but they were cheap and there were ten of them in every bag, and that was their appeal for kids like me. Most of the 45s were unexceptional, but occasionally you'd run across a diamond in the rough. That's how I found Laura Nyro's "Up On the Roof," an old Drifters song I had heard on the radio that had been written by Carole King and Gerry Goffin.

I put the 45 on the turntable, and this hauntingly beautiful voice came out of the speaker. Now I was anxious to find out what song was on the flip side. The label said "Up On the Roof," which was obviously a misprint. Curious, I dropped the needle and listened to "Captain Saint Lucifer" all the way through. My life was never the same after that. Here was someone telling her mother about an exciting new relationship with a man named Captain Saint Lucifer. Was he a real person? The devil? It didn't matter because the lyrics were like poetry: *He gives to me buckles off shingles off a cockleshell on Norway basin.*

Her second album, *Eli and the Thirteenth Confession,* was recorded in 1968. She not only wrote all the songs on the album but also produced it, sang, played piano and directed the orchestra. On the back of the album, her credits read: *piano, vocals and witness to the confession.* Who was this person? I had to know more. With an artist's eye for detail, Laura Nyro created paintings as rich as anything in the Metropolitan Museum of Art on her third album, *New York Tendaberry* with images like this: *Rugs and drapes and drugs and capes, sweet kids in hunger slums.* And this: *Firecrackers break, and they cross, and they dust, and they skate, and the night comes.*

Synesthesia is the sensory phenomenon in which musical sounds are perceived as colors, and she had the gift. I've heard stories about how she'd interrupt a musician during a recording to tell him, "I'm sorry, but that oboe is not navy enough," and he'd understand that the tone she wanted was much deeper. Or she'd tell the violin section that they weren't yellow enough, and they knew exactly what she meant. Her songs were filled with references to color. "Lu" on *Eli's Thirteenth Confession* begins: *Silver was the color, winter was the snowbell.* In another verse we hear: *Amber was the color, summer was a flameride.*

She could be ambiguous, the message not always clear, as if inviting you to intuit her meaning. In "December's Boudoir" she writes: *Loving you timelessly, love-colored soul, love-colored soul kissing spice.* Those are the words of an artist in the purest sense of the word, and I became obsessed with her. When I was still in high school, I stole a copy of *Life* magazine from the library for the photos inside of *my* idol meeting *her* idol, Miles Davis. She had asked him to sit in on one of her sessions, possibly contribute something to the record. The story goes that after he listened to her run through one of her songs, he said, "I can't play that; you've already done it all." High praise from Miles Davis, but not surprising.

Because she'd grown up in New York and was writing about life there, I decided that I had to go to New York, too. That's partly why I applied to N.Y.U. In between classes at Stella Adler, I'd go to the Upper West Side and roam the streets looking for the door on the cover of a songbook of hers I'd bought. She'd been photographed in front of that door, and I just knew I'd recognize it if I saw it, but I never did.

Years later when I was a celebrity colorist, one of my clients was Liz Rosenberg, who was Madonna's publicist. Liz had been invited to one of Laura Nyro's concerts, and she took me along. When we went backstage, I was at a loss for words.

Liz laughed. "I've never seen Brad speechless before."

I had made a silver comb to hold back her waist-length hair and engraved the words "To Laura, Love Brad" on the side. When I presented it to her, she seemed puzzled.

"I'm just a regular person," she said when I told her how much I worshipped her.

"You saved me," I insisted because she had.

So, I was hysterical when in April, 1997, I heard that she had died of ovarian cancer at forty-nine just like her mother before her. I was getting a lot of bad press at the time, and my spirits were low, but when Liz invited me to a memorial concert for the singer who had been my muse, I went. Later that night I heard the voice of God for the second time in my life: *They can't take your art from you.* I had been on the fence about leaving New York, but those words convinced me to stay.

When Laura was inducted into the Rock and Roll Hall of Fame in 2011, her son Gil Bianchini accepted the award for her, and I left him a message on Facebook. Then one afternoon I saw him coming out of the subway and decided to tell him how much his mother had meant to me and that I probably wouldn't have come to New York if it wasn't for her.

Laura was just twenty-one years old when she wrote "And When I Die," which became a big hit for both Peter, Paul and Mary and Blood, Sweat and Tears. In light of her untimely death, the lyrics seemed remarkably prescient to me: *And when I die and when I'm dead, dead and gone, there'll be one child born and a world to carry on.* Certainly, she never imagined that her only child would outlive her or that he'd become the keeper of her legacy, but that's exactly what happened.

A documentary about his mother is in the works, and Gil, who is also a singer-songwriter, will serve as associate producer. The film is based in part on the 2003 biography *Soul Picnic: The Music and Passion of Laura Nyro* by Michele Kort, which she wrote in 2012.

Growing up, there were other singers who also had an impact on me, including Todd Rundgren. I still remember seeing him on the cover of his 1974 album *Todd*, his long hair dyed at least six different shades, including pink and green. That was all the encouragement I needed to bleach my own hair and dye it blue. I loved that he was straight, yet

    Brad Johns with Marianne Dougherty

he'd show up on *Midnight Special* wearing false eyelashes, lipstick and sequins, like he was showing me what was possible, who I might become. David Bowie was another performer who blurred the line between masculine and feminine, and when he cut and dyed his hair a shocking shade of red to play the androgynous alien Ziggy Stardust, I cut and dyed my hair red, too.

It was through my boyhood friend Jeff that I discovered Joni Mitchell. I had been listening to Laura pound the piano and scream out her pain. Now here was this waif with long blonde hair softly picking out her sorrow and heartache on a grand piano, note by note. Of all her albums, *Blue* is still my favorite. "Songs are like tattoos," she sang in her clear, resonate soprano on the title song from that album, reminding us that songs which mean something to us have staying power. They get stuck in our heads. They get under our skin: *Ink on a pin underneath the skin.* When Joni Mitchell sang about "making it through these waves, acid, booze and ass, needles, guns and grass," I believed that I could make it, too.

A few years after *Blue* came out, I met Joni Mitchell, not backstage at a concert but at Jean Louis David Salon in Henri Bendel on Fifth Avenue in New York where I was working at the time. It was late in the afternoon when I went to the front desk to see if I had any other appointments that day. In the book was just one: *J. Mitchell, perm, 4 p.m.* I was hoping to go home. Now I'd have to provide a service that would take at least two hours. If I could have found someone else to give J. Mitchell that perm, I would have. So, imagine my surprise when the elevator doors opened into the reception area and out walked Joni Mitchell.

Recovering my composure, I escorted her to my chair where she chain-smoked while I worked and we talked about the album cover for *Hejira,* which featured a portrait of her taken by Norman Seeff. She is wearing a beret and a fur cape, and a cigarette smolders between her fingers. In the foreground is a two-lane blacktop, the white line down the middle disappearing into a puff of clouds.

I had admired Laura Nyro as an artist because she was involved in every aspect of her work, but Joni was just as hands-on. When she was looking for a title for the album (the songs were written while she was on a series of road trips between 1975 and 1976), she found the word *hejira,* which means exodus or migration, in the dictionary. As a proper noun, Hejira also describes Muhammad's departure from Mecca to Medina.

Collaborating with photographer Joel Bernstein, she oversaw a shoot that took place at Lake Mendota in Madison, Wisconsin, after an ice storm. In interviews, she has talked about how the album captures the "sweet loneliness of solitary travel." Certainly, each of the fourteen photographs taken in the frigid cold (she enlarged them herself using a camera lucida, an optical device used as a drawing aid by artists) that appear on the cover or on the album sleeves convey a sense of loneliness and isolation, and that's her doing.

Like all great artists, Joni Mitchell knows exactly what she wants. I'm just glad she wanted a perm that day and that I was the one to do it because it allowed me to spend all that time with her, not as a fan but as one artist to another.

5

M y mother understood that the only way out of poverty and the limited circumstances of my birth was to get an education, and she wouldn't let anything, or anyone, get in my way. One night after she'd gone to sleep, something woke her up. *A premonition?* Whatever it was, she came charging into the living room, snapped on the overhead lights and ordered my friend Debbie out of her house.

Blonde and beautiful with a cherubic face, Debbie and I had been friends since we were little, but now we were thirteen and our hormones had kicked in. My mother discovered us on the sofa, our limbs entwined. We were only kissing, which was harmless enough. I'm not sure things would have gone any further, but my mother was already imagining the worst: an unwanted pregnancy, my life ruined.

After sending Debbie home, my mother told me in no uncertain terms that I had a bright future ahead of me and that there was no way in hell she was going to allow me to become trapped in the projects like she was. This was a revelation to me since I had felt worthless for so long, but it planted a seed deep in my subconscious: *Maybe I could make something of myself.* I had always gotten good grades in school, and my teachers were supportive, but now, thanks to my mother's unwavering belief in me, I had a reason to excel.

When I was a sophomore in high school, I took acting classes at the Pittsburgh Playhouse, which is Point Park

University's Performing Arts Center. Shirley Jones studied acting there before she moved to Hollywood and starred in films like *Carousel* and *Oklahoma*. Acting appealed to me, at least in part, because it allowed me to assume a completely new identity. Onstage I wasn't Brad Johns from OVA. I was Ned Darrell in *Strange Interlude* or Edmund Tyrone in *Long Day's Journey Into Night*.

Then, in the summer of my junior year, I auditioned for and was accepted into a three-week program at Carnegie Mellon School of Drama where I was introduced to a world outside of the projects and my hometown. I met kids who'd come from New York City to study acting at CMU. For breakfast, they ate bagels and yogurt, which seemed incredibly sophisticated to me at the time. No one in OVA ate yogurt!

Before our first class, we practiced yoga to relax and create mental clarity. I learned about the way voice is produced, about vocal cords and resonators, technique and endurance. We'd practice diction with corks in our mouths. Pittsburgh has a very distinct accent, a dialect of American English brought to the area by early settlers from southern England. You don't go downtown, you go *dahntahn*. Acting classes helped me lose my Pittsburgh accent for good. I imagine that's why actors like Jeff Goldblum and Michael Keaton have no discernable Pittsburgh accent even though they grew up there just like I did.

After lunch each day, we'd break up into groups to work on a performance we were expected to give before graduation. My group was fortunate enough to study with Israel Hicks, an African American acting teacher, who worked Off Broadway and in regional theaters across the country after he left CMU, ultimately directing August Wilson's entire cycle of plays about the Black experience, which were set in Pittsburgh's Hill District.

One of my takeaways from those acting classes was that mind, body and soul are all connected. If those three elements are not in sync, you can't perform. That lesson has served me well throughout my life. Meditation, yoga, working out at the gym each day, becoming a vegetarian, honing my craft—that's what kept me at the top of my game professionally.

By the time those three weeks at CMU came to an end, I had decided to pursue acting as a career, and applied to N.Y.U. The curriculum at the N.Y.U. Tisch School of the Arts was very stringent. You studied Stanislavski, a seminal Russian theater practitioner. You studied Strindberg, the Swedish playwright. Then in 1972, the year before I graduated from high school, the Stella Adler School of Acting became affiliated with the Tisch School of the Arts, and I knew that's where I wanted to go. To be accepted into the program, I'd have to audition, but that meant going to New York City, which would be an expensive proposition.

While I was trying to figure out how I'd come up with the cash to fly to New York, my mother was busy planning a party at the VFW to celebrate my high school graduation. Since we couldn't afford to have it catered, my grandmother made all the ethnic specialties I'd grown up with, including *pierogi* (dumplings filled with cheese and potato) and *halushki* (cabbage and noodles). That night one of my mother's friends slipped me one of the diet pills they all lived on in those days. It was the first time I did speed, and I liked the way it made me feel: hyped up, talkative, happy.

Everyone who showed up (family, friends and neighbors) gave me a card with a little money tucked inside, and it was enough to buy a plane ticket to New York. I spent a lot of time choosing what to wear to my audition before settling on high-waisted bellbottoms from the Army/Navy store, a beige polyester crop top with puffed sleeves and powder-blue platform shoes with six-inch heels from Thom McAn.

Since my favorite rock band was Led Zeppelin, Robert Plant influenced my sartorial style. It was rumored that he wore women's blouses onstage. I was still trying to figure out where someone like me fit in—my looks bordered on pretty, not ruggedly handsome. Plant was straight, but he challenged our notions of what was masculine and what was feminine, and I liked that.

My audition required me to perform two monologues that demonstrated some serious acting chops as well as my comedic range, but I also had to sing a song of my choice. I chose "Buy and Sell" by Laura Nyro because the opening lyrics resonated with me at the time: *Cocaine and quiet beers, sweet candy and caramel, pass the time and dry the tears on a street called buy and sell.* Besides, I knew that Laura was from the Bronx and reasoned that the panel might think I belonged in New York too if I sang one of her songs.

When I walked off the stage, I knew I'd aced my audition. It was the first time in my life that I felt supported by something bigger than myself. Call it God, call it the universe, call it whatever you want, but something was working in my favor that day. I am absolutely certain of that. That's why it was no surprise to me when my mother handed me an envelope with an acceptance letter from New York University. My new life was about to begin.

     Brad Johns with Marianne Dougherty

6

had been praying to meet a girl who really understood me when Vivian walked into my life. The Stella Adler Studio was like a cathedral to me. I wouldn't have been surprised to see a font of holy water when I walked through the door. What I saw instead one morning in 1973 was a girl in a red shirt with a spider web made of glitter on the front, skintight Lee jeans that hugged every curve and a headful of huge, dark curls. The *piece de resistance*: a pair of red leather platforms with seven-inch wooden heels from Goody Two Shoes. Goody Two Shoes was *the* place to buy shoes you couldn't find anyplace else: silver open-toed platforms with ankle straps, glam rock heels made of solid wood with transparent tops, woven leather platform sandals.

Vivian wasn't classically beautiful. Her hair was a mass of unruly curls; her nose, in profile, less like Grace Kelly's than Barbra Streisand's, but to me she was perfect, an Egyptian queen with the exotic good looks of Cleopatra or Nefertari.

Without hesitation, I walked right up to her. "You look fabulous," I said. "I have been waiting my whole life to meet someone like you." From that moment on, we were inseparable.

Vivian came from money. Her father was an attorney who worked for the military, and she grew up in Korea and Germany where her brother was a concert pianist. Our lives couldn't have been more different, but we bonded from the beginning. When Vivian took me to a Broadway play, we sat right up front.

"Don't buy the cheap seats even if you're poor," she told me. "You could die tomorrow so use your last cent if you have to, but sit up front." That was Vivian's philosophy.

Where I may have been timid, Vivian was bold. Where I may have been fearful, Vivian was courageous, adventuresome, audacious. I learned a lot from her, including how to dress. As soon as she saw me in the fake fur green and yellow coat I'd bought at Gimbels before I left Pittsburgh, she told me to throw it out. Then she took me shopping at one of the many boutiques she frequented in those days. No one worth their platform stilettos would shop at Macy's, though they made an exception for Henri Bendel, the luxury woman's specialty store on Fifth Avenue.

None of the clothing you saw in the boutiques Vivian took me to was mass-produced. Instead, everything was carefully curated, and there were only two or three of the same item. I made a beeline to a jacket made of pony fur and calfskin. Vivian encouraged me to try it on, but the sleeves seemed way too short, and the fit was tight. Zipped to the neck, the jacket barely covered my midriff.

"That's what's in right now," Vivian assured me, and naturally I believed her.

I caught a glimpse of the price tag: $300! I had never owned an article of clothing that expensive. In high school, I'd cobbled together my wardrobe by shopping at the five-and-dime store G.C. Murphy, the bargain basement at Joseph Horne's or Claber's, a department store that sold everything at a deep discount. But Vivian made me feel special, like I was worth something, and now I was determined to find a way to own that pony fur jacket.

     Brad Johns with Marianne Dougherty

I think Vivian recognized something in me, an innate sense of style I had never been able to indulge. One day when we were out window-shopping with our friend Amber, I saw a bespoke black leather jumpsuit with wide bell-bottoms in the window of a very exclusive store on Park Avenue called T. Jones. When I glanced at Vivian, who could intuit my thoughts at that point, she suggested that we go inside.

When I came out of the dressing room, they both gasped. "That suit is so you," Amber said.

"I know," I agreed, "but I can't afford it."

Amber got to her feet. "I can," she said. "Give it to me."

When she paid for the suit in cash, Vivian and I glanced at each other. We both knew what Amber did to make that kind of money, but she was generous to a fault. Besides, who were we to judge?

Vivian dressed me up like I was her own personal Ken doll. If we were going to one of the gay clubs like 12 West, it was motorcycle boots from Harley-Davidson paired with black leather pants and matching vests. The discos required the kind of extravagant urban fashion for men you could only find at one of the boutiques near Time's Square: lime-green polyester suits, fedoras with a feather in the hat band, candy-colored faux fur coats and four-inch platforms in a range of kaleidoscopic colors. It's like I was trying on different personas, still trying to figure out who I was except that I was doing it in real life, not on the stage.

Occasionally we'd go uptown to places like Le Jardin or Xenon, but a lot of straight people went there and it was very bougie. Max's Kansas City attracted the iconoclasts: Andy Warhol's crowd, David Bowie, the New York Dolls, one of the first bands of the early punk scene. Todd Rundgren and Lou Reed came there to hang out with other rockers like them. They might be at a table having dinner together and later, if they felt like it, start jamming onstage. I met Todd's on-again-off-again girlfriend Bebe Buell there and ended up doing her hair for years. We're still friends today. Edie Sedgwick, one of Warhol's superstars, used to arrive in nothing but a fur coat and stilettos. Occasionally we'd catch a glimpse of bare tit or shoulder. Outcasts all, Max's Kansas City was our citadel.

When Vivian officially became my girlfriend, we moved out of the dorm and into an apartment near the famed Dakota, which I painted half-black and half-white with dominos on the ceiling. I had been thinking about dropping out of school for a couple of months, less certain than before that acting was my calling. I liked acting; I just didn't love it.

Stella Adler was fond of saying, "Your choice is your talent," and I reasoned that if I wasn't going to be a great actor, I'd made the wrong choice. I was also starting to wonder if I wanted to be someone else onstage every night when I still hadn't figured out who I was.

When I announced that I might move back to Pittsburgh until I knew what I wanted to do with my life, Vivian put her foot down. Insisting that I belonged in New York, she suggested beauty school since I used to cut and color everyone's hair in the dorms when we lived there.

The Robert Fiance Hair Design Institute still enjoys a reputation as one of the finest cosmetology schools in the country with alumni that includes the colorist Louis Licari as well as Cyndi Lauper and Debi Mazar, who were hairdressers before they became celebrities. When I showed up for my interview in head-to-toe leather and inhaled the seductive chemical odor of perm solution, I had such a visceral reaction that I knew at once that I had found my calling.

7

Once I started beauty school, my world became a con- cocted world. Black Beauties were a stimulant that kept me focused in class, but speed is like gasoline; it stays in your system for days. So, to take the edge off around four o'clock, I'd ingest half a Tuinal, which was marketed as a sedative to help with insomnia when it was introduced in the 1940s. You can't get it anymore.

You have to understand that a world of mind-altering substances was as real to me as anything I'd ever experienced, maybe better than what most people call real life. A world without drugs was a world I simply did not want to live in.

If I wanted to go out dancing and stay up all night, a different combination of drugs was required. Before we went downtown, a group of my friends would come over to my apartment for *hor d'oeuvres*: cocaine and heroin in powdered form and MDA (a recreational drug in the same class as psychedelics) that we served in silver salt cellars on silver trays with silver spoons from Tiffany.

I did drugs with an upper echelon of people who came from privilege and could afford to shop at Tiffany. If we went to a party at someone else's apartment where the coke was served on a dinner plate with a paper straw, we declined, not the drugs but the method of delivery. Someone would pull a crisp one-hundred-dollar bill from their wallet, roll it up and snort the coke that way. Presentation was everything and just as important as the high.

I was still confused about my sexuality, and when I went home for Christmas that year, I saw my high school girlfriend. A couple of months later, she called to tell me that she was pregnant. I knew that if we got married and raised a child together that I'd have to leave New York and move back to Pittsburgh where I'd be trapped just like my mother had been in OVA.

While it was a relief when she decided to terminate the pregnancy, it was one of those bittersweet fork-in-the-road moments that leave you pondering the what-ifs. That winter I went back to Pittsburgh to see her one last time. The sky was overcast and dreary, and when I left her apartment, it felt like a door had closed on the life I might have lived. My life, for better or worse, was in New York now.

Meanwhile, aside from the amphetamines and the coke, I was also doing angel dust, the street name for PCP, a hallucinogen that works as a stimulant and can cause hallucinations, agitation, mania and irrational thinking. Like Ketamine, which is a short-acting general anesthetic, PCP had been used to tranquilize large animals; hence the street name *hog*. It can also block memory, emotions or pain. So, there's that.

I'd heard about junkies like jazz musicians Charlie Parker and Stan Getz, but they were shooting heroin. I was taking pills, which we got from a doctor. How could that be so bad? Vivian tried to get me to slow down, but I wouldn't listen to her, and we started fighting about stupid things. I rarely ate so I lost about twenty-five pounds, and I was getting almost no sleep. If I ran out of Tuinals, I'd become frantic, searching through the pockets of every jacket I owned. I was taking so many of them that I'd fall down on the dance floor or on the sidewalk. Before long I was covered with bruises.

The night I collapsed at Infinity was a reckoning of sorts. When the cabbie dropped us off at the curb, the doorman on duty that night helped Vivian get me up to our apartment and into bed.

"Looks like you had a little too much fun last night," he said when I saw him the next day.

Maybe it looked like fun to him, and it was for a long while, until it wasn't. Viv and I were fighting all the time, and it was getting harder and harder to stay coherent when I called my mother, who sensed I was in trouble after I slurred my way through an entire conversation. When she informed me in no uncertain terms that *they* were coming to get me, I knew who she meant.

My father and grandfather drove to New York a few days later in a beat-up, wood-paneled station wagon. The broken windows in the backseat had been covered in plastic that did little to keep out the frigid cold. It was a long drive, and they stayed in a cheap motel in an iffy neighborhood the night they arrived. The next morning, certain that Vivian would try to stop me from going with them, they waited until they saw her leave for school before hustling me out to the car.

If I was going to be rehabilitated, I'd have to wean myself off the drugs, and I knew just how to do it from what I'd read in the *Physician's Desk Reference.* So, I left New York with an empty vitamin bottle full of the drugs I'd need to withdraw and slept all the way back to Pittsburgh. When my father woke me up, I was disoriented. At first, I had no idea where I was. Then, slowly, it dawned on me that I was home.

— 8 —

My parents had finally moved out of OVA to a house across the river, but there were only three bedrooms: one for them, one for Craig and one for Shari. I moved in with my grandmother. I knew she was lonely, and we became best friends during those long months I spent with her. Most nights we'd watch television, usually a movie featuring some actor she liked. Her favorite was Guy Madison, who I remembered from the TV show *The Adventures of Wild Bill Hickok* that was popular in the 1950s.

"I love Guy Madison, but I also loved Rudolph Valentino," she told me. Then she giggled. "Don't tell your grandfather. He'd be jealous if he knew."

When he was young, my grandfather bore a passing resemblance to Rudolph Valentino, but in real life he was nothing like the matinee idol my grandmother thought was so handsome. I had not forgotten that he used a racial slur to describe The Supremes, who I adored.

If you had asked me if I planned to resume my old life in New York once I got clean, I wouldn't have had an answer for you. Addicts don't think that far ahead. Like Buddhists, addicts live in the present. When you're deep into your addiction, like I was, all you think about is drugs, and I thought about them all day. I loved the colors they came in: the baby-blue Amytal capsules, which knocked you out, and the bright orange-red Seconals that kept you knocked out. That's what killed Marilyn Monroe. Tuinal was a combination of both.

For those first couple of weeks at my grandmother's house, I slowly weaned myself off the drugs, and it was brutal. There is a set of symptoms you experience when you stop using barbiturates, and I had them all: cramping and nausea, vomiting and diarrhea, agitation and anxiety. One night I fell out of bed, and my grandmother rushed into my bedroom where she found me on the floor. I'm not sure what she thought, but if she suspected that her favorite grandson was a junkie going through withdrawal, she never let on, and I am grateful for that.

I was convinced that it was my responsibility to accumulate enough wealth to provide for my parents and siblings, and beauty school offered a way out of poverty, a pathway to a lucrative career if I worked hard enough. So, I enrolled at Pittsburgh Beauty Academy (PBA), one of the top beauty schools in the country at the time.

I took a bus downtown every morning just like my aunt Alice did to go to her job at Mellon Bank, and I loved my teachers, but the long bus ride home each day during rush hour was grueling. My kit was heavy, and I had to wedge it between my feet. A cosmetology student's kit is the size of a small suitcase and holds everything they need to practice their craft: mannequin heads, blow-dryers, clippers, brushes and combs, scissors and razors, capes and aprons, sprays, gel, perm rods, rollers, vinyl gloves and tint bowls.

Each day when I got home from school, I'd pour myself a glass of iced tea, carry the green plastic tumbler onto the front porch and sit on the glider, which was like a swing but on a fixed frame. I'd kept a stash of drugs "just in case," and I allowed myself one Tuinal per day. Fall and winter are the worst times of year for me because the lack of sunlight exacerbates my depression, and during those bleak, dreary months in Pittsburgh, Tuinal became my light.

Because PBA accepted some of the credits I'd accrued at Robert Fiance, I graduated in six months, but I had no intention of staying in Pittsburgh. New York was like a siren call to me, both powerful and seductive. When I told my mother that I was leaving, there was sadness in her eyes.

"I'd rather be a junkie with a needle in my arm than keep living here," I told her because I knew that my future was in New York.

That August I packed up my things and left Pittsburgh, for good this time. A new chapter in my life was beginning, but it was still unclear how that chapter would end. Would I start doing drugs again once I was back in the city? I wasn't sure of anything except that it was time for me to start making some serious money.

My first real job was at Cinandre, which occupied three whole floors of a building on East 57th Street. The décor was white with touches of red and blue, the name a mash-up of syllables from the first names of the original owners: Francine Berg and Andre Martheleur, who was not only a hairdresser but also an artist and photographer. He and Jamaican model Grace Jones were a couple, and one day I saw her having a pedicure while Andre painted her body for a photo shoot.

Hairdressers were like gods in those days, and everyone who was rich or famous went to Cinandre, including John F. Kennedy, Jr. Celebrity hairdresser Edward Tricomi's first job was at Cinandre, which he called the "Studio 54 of Hair." His first client: Salvador Dali.

Andre pioneered a groundbreaking technique for doing perms, using rollers instead of rods, which produced more natural results. He called it a retexturizing service, and women loved it because they could shampoo their hair and let it air-dry. Then when the back-to-nature movement went mainstream, we started using henna, which is harvested from a plant and seemed like a healthier alternative to hair dye. I ladled it out of barrels that were shipped in from Egypt and mixed it with water for clients like the model Dayle Haddon, who was the most beautiful woman I'd ever seen.

Don Matthews, the color director at Cinandre, became a mentor. He taught me about the science of hair color, how to bleach and tone hair like they did in the 1950s. Don was a celebrity colorist before the expression had even been coined. Lauren Hutton, Gloria Vanderbilt, Martha Graham and the actress Pauline Goddard paid $55 to have their hair "streaked" by the master.

I began experimenting with food dye and cornstarch to add a temporary wash of color in unconventional colors like blue and green to bleached hair. It was like being back in my grandmother's kitchen mixing up a batch of blue taffy, and Andy Warhol's people loved it.

I met the legendary makeup artists Sandy Linter and Wendy Whitelaw at Cinandre. Wendy was one of the best makeup artists I ever knew, every bit as good as Way Bandy, the highest-paid makeup artist in the world at the time. I used to see her at the Mudd Club made up like the Grady twins in *The Shining*: black baby-doll dress with puffy sleeves, black Mary Janes, black lipstick and black nail color.

Sandy was having a much-publicized affair with the supermodel Gia Caranji, who she met at a photo shoot for

Harper's Bazaar Italia in 1978. All the major fashion magazines hired Sandy and Wendy to work with them. Models were treated like commodities in those days, and when Gia started showing up at fashion shoots high on heroin, everyone from editors to photographers looked the other way. The 1980 cover of *Vogue* was controversial because you can see the track marks on her arms. Her heroin addiction derailed her career, and she died of AIDS at the age of twenty-six. Jade Hobson, the former fashion director at *Vogue,* has admitted that models like Gia who were actively using drugs were exploited.

Drugs were just part of the culture in those days, and everyone came to work high on something: marijuana or a little coke. Clients used to tip me by slipping a bag of cocaine into my pocket. When I came to work one day zoned out on Tuinal, someone suggested that I should "take it easy." So, I learned how to compartmentalize, putting the junkie in a box on my left shoulder on weekdays when I was working and letting him out on the weekend.

We worked with a lot of models, and most of them were pressured to sleep with the photographer if they wanted to work. It was an unwritten code that also applied to gay hairdressers like me who feared losing their jobs if they didn't sleep with the salon owner or the color director or anyone else who had the power to have them fired. It was like survival of the fittest, and there was always someone willing to exploit someone less powerful than them. Don Matthews never crossed that line even though he wielded at lot of power.

I had worked for a small salon on the Upper East Side before coming to Cinandre, and I remember the sense of dread I felt when my boss invited me to have dinner at his apartment. I drank a lot of Johnny Walker Black with him that night to steel myself for what came next. The sex was painful and bloody, and I grabbed a red velour pillow and cried into it while he fucked me.

That night I vowed that if I was ever in a position of power, I'd never take advantage of anyone like that, and it's a promise I've kept to this day.

9

When I was growing up my mother and I used to watch *Hollywood Squares*. Paul Lynde was one of the celebrity panelists, whose campy persona and dry wit hinted that he might be gay. There was never anything explicit, though when asked on the show if the electrical current in his house was AC or DC, he famously replied, "In my house, it's both!" Long before Lady Gaga wrote a song that expressed the same sentiment, my mother pointed to Paul Lynde, who occupied the center square, and announced that there are people, like him, who are "born that way, but it's okay."

Maybe she was giving me permission to be whatever I wanted to be. So, what did *she* want? I know she imagined a big life for me just as she had once imagined a big life for my father. I also knew that she believed marriage was a trap that would derail those plans. She may have reasoned that if I was gay, I'd never end up married and saddled with kids like she was.

I hadn't given my own sexuality much thought at that point. In fourth grade I had a crush on my teacher Mr. Raymond, who was movie-star handsome. He was always immaculately dressed in a white shirt, gray suit and tie, and when he walked in the room, everything seemed brighter. He liked me because I was a good student, and when he praised me in front of my classmates, I felt a sense of pride as if I mattered.

In fifth grade, I developed a crush on Miss Cheroke. She was my Ann-Margret: copper-colored hair she wore in a bouffant, green eyes and fair skin. Because I was drawn to color ever since I was a child, I noticed that she wore a lot of green: tight shift dresses made of lame, a fabric woven with ribbons of metallic fiber. Her family owned a trucking company in Pittsburgh so she didn't need to work, but she loved teaching, and I was her pet. After a while I started bringing little gifts to school for her, maybe a bottle of nail polish in a shade I thought she'd like or a magazine with a fashion spread that included a dress just like one she had worn to school. I wanted her to know that I loved her, and I did.

The truth is, Mr. Raymond turned me on, but so did Miss Cheroke. We didn't use the word bisexual then to describe what I was feeling. Though I had dated plenty of girls in high school, I found that I was attracted to a guy with long black hair I saw at N.Y.U. one day who looked just like Johnny Thunders, the guitar player for The New York Dolls. So, I walked right up to him and asked if he'd go out with me. He made it clear that he preferred girls, but I didn't see what difference that made. I just wanted to hang out with him.

Vivian and I were having lunch in the cafeteria one day when I noticed a gorgeous guy who reminded me of the actor Don Johnson. I'd just seen him in a film called *The Harrad Experiment*. It would be another decade before he'd play Sonny Crockett on *Miami Vice*. When I told Viv I was going to go over and say hello, she shook her head, code for "He's straight."

I ignored her and introduced myself anyway. "Would you like to have dinner with me?"

When the answer was an emphatic, "No," I wasn't offended, just not sure what the problem was. Girls. Boys. I didn't see the distinction.

The first time I fooled around with a guy was at N.Y.U. I'd seen him in acting class and knew that he had a roommate, who was straight but also questioning his sexuality just like I was. One night we got high at someone's apartment, and some of our friends encouraged us to go into one of the bedrooms together just to see what happened. Neither of us had ever been with another man before, but when you're stoned you do a lot of things you might not do otherwise. To my surprise, I found that I liked kissing him. To tell the truth, I would have been happy if that's all we did. I'd masturbated before but had never touched another man that way, but when I touched him, he came almost immediately before apologizing profusely. I don't think we did much more than that. Still, it was the first time I'd been with a man and I liked it.

Here's the thing: It was never just about the sex for me, though it was for a lot of other people who hooked up for sex with strangers in public bathrooms or gay bathhouses across the city. In the 1970s, New York City was a mecca for gay kids who had grown up in small towns in the Midwest where they were ostracized or bullied for being different, but here they could flaunt their sexuality, and they did. I wasn't into cruising or anonymous sex. I wanted to fall in love. So, when Vivian and I went to the clubs, I was on the dance floor like Sandra Dee looking for "the one," while everyone else just wanted to bang each other in a bathroom stall.

I met this pretty Puerto Rican guy from Queens at a club one night and went home with him. He was very attentive, and the sex was good. The whole experience felt romantic

     Brad Johns with Marianne Dougherty

to me, and by the time I left I was already envisioning our future together. "I have a boyfriend now," I told myself on the subway going back to Manhattan.

I called him three days in a row before he finally picked up. "Why do you keep calling me?" He sounded irritated.

I told him that I wanted to see him again. After all, we'd spent most of the next day together, and there had been a connection; I was sure of it. His brushoff—he never had sex more than once with anyone no matter how much he liked them—was heartless and cruel for someone like me who knew nothing about how the gay world operated. There was no manual. I was flying blind here with no one to teach me the rules, if there were rules. Were meaningless one-night stands the best I could hope for from now on?

I knew I wanted more than that, but I seemed to have gotten it all wrong. It was a very confusing time for me, and somehow intimacy got tangled up with the fear of being abandoned, or worse, trapped like my mother. Opening your heart to someone was to risk rejection, to be vulnerable, and that scared me.

When I was too afraid to go the distance with someone who really loved me, relationships became complicated and messy. Obsessed with my career, I kept everyone at arm's length. None of my lovers stayed overnight. Instead, they went home before the sun came up because *I had to work.*

— **10** —

Vivian and I were still technically boyfriend and girlfriend in 1976, but I'd made a decision. From now on I'd only go out with men. Since they wouldn't expect anything of me (marriage, children), I could focus on my career. It was a peculiar kind of logic that made sense to me at the time, but breaking up with Vivian was the hardest thing I ever did. It felt like choosing sides, but I saw no other option.

She wasn't mad, just hurt, but she understood. Then fate stepped in and changed her life, sending her down a road I could never have walked with her. About five years after our breakup, Vivian went to Hawaii for a family vacation. When she got an upgrade from coach to first class, she found herself seated next to a very attractive man named Robert. By the time the plane landed in Honolulu, they had exchanged phone numbers and made plans to see each other in New York when they got home.

"I think I met the man I'm going to marry," Vivian told me when she got back.

It was a bittersweet moment because I knew that our relationship would change with Robert in the picture, and it did, though not in ways I could have imagined. After all these years, we are family: Viv, Robert, their two grown children and me.

Vivian might have found the love of her life, and I was happy for her, but I had yet to meet mine. In retrospect,

     Brad Johns with Marianne Dougherty

I'm not sure I would have known what to do if I did. I was a young, bitchy queen in those days, but that was just a defense mechanism to keep anyone from getting too close. Hadn't my mother told me that love was a trap?

Raul changed everything. I met him at Ice Palace 57, a gay disco on 57th Street with a six-dollar cover charge and lots of neon and mirrors. I'd gone there for one of their Sunday tea dances with my friend Adam, who worked at Cinandre with me.

Raul was from Puerto Rico and lived in the Bronx with his extended family. Adam and I were at the bar when he approached us and struck up a conversation. I had never seen anyone as beautiful as Raul: wavy golden curls, a sandy mustache and emerald-green eyes that reminded me of tourmaline. Depending on the tilt of his head, they registered slight changes in composition, becoming a maelstrom of whirling green and gold leaf when he laughed.

When he asked me to dance, I noticed that he was wearing dirty Converse sneakers. There was something so endearing about those beat-up Chuck Taylors that I couldn't help falling in love with him. We danced together for a long time and made out in the dark on the bleachers. When we went home together that night, I was worried that he'd want to have sex and that it might be painful, but Raul was sensitive and romantic.

For the next couple of years, we were inseparable. We didn't have to do anything special; it was enough just to be together. Sometimes I'd visit him in the Bronx, and we'd go to the park just to hang out. Ever since I was a little boy, I'd felt terrified each morning when I woke up. Not Raul. Raul was genuinely happy when he woke up, and after a while his happiness was contagious. Now I was happy too.

Raul worked as a hairdresser and makeup artist in Bronxville, but he could do anything: cut, color, styling. He was like Serge Lutens, the French photographer, hair stylist and fashion designer that way. While he dreamed of doing editorial work in Manhattan, his aesthetic was deemed "Caribbean tacky," and no one would hire him. It would be more than a decade before Jennifer Lopez would change our perception of Latinos in popular culture, and her image was crafted by a Cuban-born American hairstylist named Oribe. Timing is everything.

Our relationship was not without its problems. I had been brought up in Crazyville where my mother could fly into rages without warning, beating Shari for some infraction or the other or hurling a stream of invectives at my father. Like her, my mood could darken almost imperceptibly. When that happened, I'd start an argument with Raul over something insignificant and things would escalate quickly until I was screaming at him.

It felt like there was something wrong with my brain, like the circuitry needed rewiring, yet Raul saw through my posturing, showing compassion for the frightened little boy inside and waiting for the storm to pass.

Raul idolized Iris Chacon, the popular Puerto Rican singer, dancer and entertainer, and his nickname for me was a diminutive of her name: *Chaconcita.*

"Let me take you home, *Chaconcita*," he'd say, fixing me with one of his sweet smiles, "and I'll hold you in my arms."

One thing we looked forward to was spending the entire month of August with Raul's parents in Bayamon, a suburb of San Juan in the northern coastal valley. On our first visit,

     Brad Johns with Marianne Dougherty

Raul took me to Old San Juan where buildings dated from the sixteenth century and houses in vivid colors lined the cobblestone streets. The Spanish explorer Ponce de Leon is buried in the Cautista Cathedral.

"I have a surprise for you," Raul told me as we approached a beautiful café overlooking the harbor. A waiter showed us to a table where Raul ordered each of us a slushy concoction that tasted like ice cream laced with 180 proof rum.

"It's a pina colada," he explained. "They were invented here."

The story goes that in 1954 a bartender named Ramon "Monchito" Marrera created the legendary cocktail at the Caribe Hilton when he mixed up a batch of rum, coconut cream and pineapple juice.

Raul ordered rice and beans for each of us, which was a good thing since those pina coladas packed a punch, and we sat there for hours until the setting sun cast an orange glow on the sailboats in the harbor.

Taking my hand, Raul thanked me for spending time with him in the place where he grew up. "I don't know for sure yet," he said, "but I don't think I've ever loved anyone as much as I love you right now."

I felt the same way yet I was afraid to tell him. Somehow, I had made the assumption that people like me didn't deserve love, at least not the kind of love Raul was offering. And what if he changed his mind? What if he left me? How would I recover?

Finally, I worked up the courage to be honest with him. "Raul, I love you too, but I'm afraid of losing you."

"You won't," he reassured me, taking my hand. "We are a team in every way."

We settled the bill and looked for a cab. It's been decades since I saw Raul, but I have relived that moment with him in the backseat of a cab in Old San Juan many times since then—the stolen kisses, the warmth of his hand in mine—and wished that things might have turned out differently.

On our last visit to Puerto Rico, Raul took me aside to tell me that he did not plan on returning to New York the next morning. "This is my home."

He tried to convince me to stay. We'd open a hair and makeup studio, he said, and make a life together, but New York was *my* home now, and I couldn't do it. My career was taking off, and I was starting to make real money. Hadn't I promised to take care of my family? Staying in Puerto Rico with Raul seemed like too big a risk. So, I let him go.

After our breakup, I became a totally different person, chopping off my long shag haircut, buzzing my hair and bleaching it white. I bought an expensive new wardrobe of fringed Ralph Lauren Western wear. Maybe I wanted to be someone else when I looked in the mirror, not the person who fucked it up with the love of his life.

For the first time, I started going out to clubs by myself, secretly wishing that someone would hurt or even kill me, ending my miserable life. Like all the heartbroken, lonely people in the world, I thought I'd never love anyone else again and was naïve enough to believe that each of us has only one true love per lifetime. I was wrong about that, but I was also a hopeless romantic.

My downward spiral in thousands of dollars-worth of new clothes lasted for about a year. The point had been to look hot so I could attract guys, but somehow that no longer seemed important, and I started going out dressed in ripped jeans and a T-shirt. One night at The Village Stix, a gay bar on Second Avenue, I met Jonathan, who crossed the room to tell me that he thought I was beautiful.

Literally tall, dark and handsome, Jonathan had olive skin, hazel eyes and a mustache that was kind of sexy, not sleazy. I learned that he had a good job with the airlines, but what he didn't tell me was that he was married. I found that out much later. That night though when he drove me home, he didn't ask to come upstairs with me. Instead, like a perfect gentleman, he kissed me on the cheek and said he'd like to see me again.

If Raul had taught me how to be gay, how to have sex so it wasn't painful, how to feel deeply for someone, I taught Jonathan those things, and he was a willing pupil. It's like he was a piece of clay that I could mold to my liking. *Kiss me this way, not that way. Make love like this, not that.* One weekend he invited me to his apartment in Brooklyn. I found out later that his wife was out of town. When I asked who the woman was in framed photographs all over the house, he confessed that he was married.

The news felt like a stomach punch, but it didn't end our relationship. Jonathan admitted that he had never been with a man before me, but he had been curious for a long time about what it would be like. Eventually, his wife found out, and because he had nowhere else to go, he moved in with me. I had my own apartment on 12th Street that I hadn't bothered to furnish, though there might have been two chairs in the living room next to a stack of record albums.

I had never lived with a man before and wasn't sure I wanted to, but he couldn't move in with his parents, who had a place in Brooklyn, because they were uncomfortable with his new lifestyle. That's when I realized how lucky I was to have a family like mine.

I'd been with Jonathan for about a year when we began hearing about this disease people were calling "gay pneumonia" because so many gay men had it. By 1983 New York City had 1,000 reported AIDS cases, and that was just the beginning. Within four years, 70,000 New Yorkers were infected. For that reason alone, I was glad to be in a monogamous relationship, but Jonathan felt differently. Having just come out, he wanted to experience a gay life-style that included threesomes and anonymous sex at the city's bathhouses.

"There's a plague out there," I reminded him, but he didn't care.

Since he was still working for the airlines and flying international, it became easy to cheat on me, and like a sailor with a girl in every port, Jonathan began seeing other people in cities all over the world. Ultimately, that's what ended our relationship. Later, after he was transferred to Washington, D.C., he called to tell me that he had oral thrush, which is one of the first symptoms of HIV. He sounded excited, like he was happy to be part of the club.

When he was diagnosed with HIV, Jonathan told me that I should get tested. Vivian was pregnant with her first child, and I had been promoted to color director at Clive Summers. Now this. It took three weeks to get the results, and they were the worst three weeks of my life. It's the first thing I thought about when I woke up each morning. Even though I had been entertaining the notion of suicide since I was six, this was not the way I wanted my life to end.

It felt like a reprieve when the test results came back negative. My friend Chris and I had worked together for years. He cut hair, I colored it, and we had become as close as brothers.

"I want to be your working partner for a long time," I told him. "Let's make some rules so we don't get this disease."

     Brad Johns with Marianne Dougherty

He agreed at once, and we came up with a list. First, when we went to a bar or restaurant, we wouldn't drink out of a glass since we couldn't be certain that they were clean. Instead, we'd ask for a plastic cup or order beer in a glass bottle. I hate beer, but that's how desperate we were. We also decided that if we engaged in oral sex, we wouldn't swallow. We knew so little then about how this disease was transmitted and only learned much later that simply having ejaculate in your mouth was enough to acquire HIV, especially if you had any cuts or ulcers.

As sketchy as they were, those rules kept us alive. Jonathan wasn't so lucky. We were no longer a couple when I heard that he was living with his parents in Brooklyn where he was in the late stages of this insidious disease. When I asked if I could visit him, he said he didn't want me or anyone else to see him looking "this way."

Then in 1990 I heard from Raul, who had opened a studio with his new boyfriend and was doing hair and makeup for his idol, Iris Chacon. He asked me if I'd come for a visit; he had something to tell me. I asked Chris to go with me because I was so nervous. What could be so important that Raul couldn't tell me over the phone? I remember that it was unbearably hot the day Chris and I went to the beach to wait for Raul, yet here was this figure dressed in black with a long beard heading toward us.

Chris had an uneasy feeling. "I think that's Raul."

He was right, though I had trouble believing it. Over lunch Raul told me that he had AIDS. He had been living with the disease for a long time, but now he sensed that time was running out.

It was Vivian who told me that Raul was gone. She loved him, possibly even more than I did, and had stayed in touch. She just happened to call his parents the day Raul was dying. That's how we found out.

I hadn't cried since I was five years old and realized that I had to be the adult in the family in order to protect my baby brother. I guess I'd taken Melissa Manchester's advice to heart even before she thought of writing that song, "Don't Cry Out Loud." I had simply learned how to suck it up, push down my feelings and get on with it. I cry all the time now. I cry when I read stories about pedophilia or someone harming a defenseless animal. I cry if someone tells me they don't love me anymore. I cry when my sister tells me a sad story about her childhood. Back then, I bottled it all up, and it would be years before I'd find the courage to look inside and face my worst fears.

11

ire Island, a cigar-shaped piece of land in the Atlantic Ocean near the southern side of Long Island, New York, has a rich history in the gay and lesbian community. As far back as the 1930s, actors, writers and theater people who lived in New York City found a safe haven there in towns like Cherry Grove and Fire Island Pines. Thus, its nickname: *Chelsea with sand.* In the 1980s as a rare and often fatal form of cancer ravaged the gay community in New York, the barrier island became synonymous with AIDS, but when I started going there with Raul in 1978, we went to Fire Island to lie in the sun all day and dress for afternoon "tea dances" where no one drank tea but everyone was high on something: alcohol, speed, coke, whatever.

Our favorite tea dance was at the Ice Palace, a hotel in Cherry Grove with a pool and a dance floor on the roof. It was just a bunch of queens dressed like they were having High Tea at Buckingham Palace, but it was fun, and we danced all night to disco hits like "Last Dance" by Donna Summer or "Shame" by Evelyn "Champagne" King, who was discovered while singing as she cleaned the restrooms at Columbia Records. Raul and I loved "Boogie Oogie Oogie" by A Taste of Honey, which along with Donna Summer's "I Love You," became our song.

Drugs were a big part of the scene then, and we did a lot of them: coke, methamphetamines, and nitrous oxide, which was a colorless gas used for sedation that we sprayed on a cotton bandana and inhaled. I have a vivid memory of being in someone's swimming pool in Cherry Grove: tan, slim, a Margarita in one hand, surrounded by friends. That's why I liked drugs. They shut off the tape that ran through my head in a loop: *You're ugly. You're poor. Your boyfriend is better looking than you. Everybody wants him.*

I was not making any real money in 1978, and neither was Raul, so we took the ferry to Fire Island from Sayville, New York, on Long Island. On weekends the ferry was mobbed with gay men happy to be leaving the city for a place where they could be themselves without fear of retribution. In Cherry Grove, we'd lather ourselves in sunscreen and lie on the beach for hours, then rinse off and take a small boat to the Pines in time for the afternoon tea dance. At seven p.m. we'd move on to another tea dance that went on well into the night. The last ferry left for New York at two a.m. so if you missed that one you were out of luck. Years later, I had enough money to charter a sea plane that dropped me and a few friends off in Manhattan at 23rd near the East River, but in those days when Raul and I missed that last ferry back to the city, we slept on the beach all night.

After Raul decided to stay in Puerto Rico, I started going to Fire Island with Jonathan. We were doing so many drugs by then that we'd be on the ferry going back to Manhattan and I'd ask him if we had a good time. I presume I was having a ball while on drugs; I just couldn't remember any of it. By then AIDS had begun to cast a pall over the island where you might see someone on the beach with tell-tale purple lesions on his face or legs from Kaposi's sarcoma, a common cancer in people with HIV. I was so afraid of getting AIDS that I never had sex with anyone on Fire Island.

     Brad Johns with Marianne Dougherty

I didn't touch anything I feared might be contaminated. I went there to get high and dance, my two favorite things because they made me feel like a little child without a care in the world.

That year I was taking a lot of Ecstasy, a stimulant that alters mood and perception; so was everyone else I knew. One summer when I went to Fire Island with my friend Chris, we took Ecstasy as soon as we boarded the water taxi for the Pines. Maybe we thought there was no time to waste, but it seemed important that we feel the effects by the time we arrived. As luck (or bad luck) would have it, the water taxi broke down. Chris was the first to feel the Ecstasy kicking in, but there we were, stuck on a water taxi for another two hours, no dance floor in sight.

It was fairly popular for two gay men to bring a few beautiful girls along to Fire Island with them. The straight men must have been happy to have someone to hit on at parties. Vivian came along with me and Chris a number of times. Invariably, the girls would throw up after taking Ecstasy. I'm not sure why. Maybe it mixed poorly with their hormones. We'd let them get it out of their system and then go dancing.

My wardrobe was carefully curated in those days. One season I wore only black and white leather to the tea dances or house parties on Fire Island: hot pants or sleeveless vests that zipped up the side which I designed myself and a leathermaker in New York made to my specifications. In that respect, I was channeling my father, who had made that baby-blue suit he wore to jazz clubs in Pittsburgh when he and my mother were first married. Like I said, we may have been poor, but my parents were rich in style.

One summer I wore a different bathing suit each day One of my favorites was a leopard-print Norma Kamali for

Men bikini that I paired with a sleeveless black undershirt we called a "wife-beater." The term has been in use since 1947, but has recently been deemed offensive for obvious reasons and gone out of fashion. Chris, who was my sartorial equal in those days, wore a glow-in-the-dark "wife-beater" and a glow-in-the-dark Speedo to a party where he knew we'd be dancing under a blacklight.

Five years after I'd first gone to Fire Island with Raul, the four of us (Chris, Viv, our friend Joelle and me) rented a house in Ocean Grove, which is a community of mostly straight and very wealthy people. We spent one summer there, but got thrown out because we had too many parties. I'd gotten a taste of the Pines when I went there with Raul, and it had made a huge impression on me: the dunes and beach grass, the eerie quiet (no cars allowed), the narrow paths that lead to the ocean, the mysterious shadblow trees and one-hundred-year-old oaks in the Sunken Forest, the pitch pines and thickets of black cherry and highbush blueberry. A lot of gay men who'd made it—doctors, lawyers, fashion designers—had houses in the Pines. The fashion people invited their models out for the weekend. Madonna and her brother, who is gay, went there in the '80s. You'd see them at tea dances in Cherry Grove.

In retrospect, those were the best years of my life, but nothing lasts forever. I met Joanna, a petite, almost impish looking blonde, while I was working for Clive Summers. A millionaire married to a gay man, Joanna had two beautiful blonde children and a wealthy boyfriend. We became very close, more like brother and sister than colorist and client. She invited me to her six-bedroom, wood-frame house every weekend for the next ten summers. My mother, who visited a couple of times, was convinced that the huge old mansion was haunted. Maybe it was. Joanna knew everyone. We used to joke that she was the "official fag hag of the Pines."

I was very busy at the salon on Saturday, but I left for Fire Island as soon as I was done with my last client so we could go dancing that night. Joanna gave me my own room; no one else could stay in that room but me. Invariably, when I arrived, there would be at least $2,000 worth of drugs under the bedspread: Ecstasy, marijuana, coke, angel dust.

Most weekends Joanna threw elaborate dinner parties. She'd start cooking around six, and a group of us would eat around a big table before going out to dance. I remember one evening in particular: I had taken speed, which gave me a heightened sense of awareness. Glancing around the table, I was struck by the thought that none of these people had long to live. Some had AIDS, others were abusing very dangerous drugs. That was the first time I saw Joanna doing Ketamine or K, a dissociative anesthetic that can cause hallucinations.

Not long after that, I heard that Joanna committed suicide. She had returned all the hair jewelry I'd ever made for her in a sad little envelope with my name in her left-handed script on the front: *brad*. I never went to Fire Island again.

— 12 —

Suicide seemed so sweet when I was six. Music and my grandmother's unconditional love kept the demons at bay for a while. Later, drugs did the trick, but I'd given myself an ultimatum: if life didn't get any better by my thirtieth birthday, I'd end things.

In the summer of 1985 as the date of my impending suicide closed in, New York City was the place to be if you were in fashion or the arts. As Color Director at Clive Summers Salon in Olympic Tower, I was at the epicenter of that world with invitations to exclusive events like a party Andy Warhol threw in 1982 for artist Niki de Saint Phalle's new fragrance collection at La Couple, a branch of the famed Parisian brasserie. The glass bottles were blue, my favorite color, and the stopper featured two entwined snakes.

It was no secret that Andy had grown up in Pittsburgh just like me so I walked over to introduce myself. "Hi, Andy, I'm Brad," I told him. "I'm also from Pittsburgh."

"That's too bad," he said, fixing me with one of his trademark looks—dispassionate, impenetrable. Then, almost as an afterthought, he added, "Nice to meet you."

I made a point of getting to the salon before everyone else so I'd be ready when my first client walked in the door. One morning, a bevy of beautiful models in disheveled evening wear and smudged makeup poured out of a limo onto the sidewalk just as I arrived. Like bees in a hive, they

      Brad Johns with Marianne Dougherty

swarmed around a tall, slender man in a white suit and black turtleneck. It was obvious that they had been out all night, probably at Studio 54. As their entourage swept into the building, he and I exchanged the briefest of glances, but I felt as if I'd been singled out by someone important.

"That's Halston," Clive told me later. "His office is right upstairs."

It might seem ludicrous that I was contemplating suicide when I had a dream job in the most exciting city in the world, but when I wasn't high, I was overwhelmed by a crippling sadness that had followed me into adulthood. Now people all over the city were dying of AIDS. I knew my boyfriend was cheating on me and reasoned that it was only a matter of time before he'd get the disease and pass it on to me. Both of those things reinforced my notion that life was not worth living and suicide was my only option.

I'd been talking about nothing else for months and told all of my friends exactly how I'd do it. My apartment was decorated in warm earth tones like chestnut, caramel and russet. I'd simply slash my wrists, lie down on the plush carpet and bleed out surrounded by all that warmth.

So, why am I still here? I've come to think of what happened next as divine intervention, an act of God. I came into work one morning where my handsome, green-eyed Argentinian assistant was waiting for me. Impulsively, I told him to cancel all my appointments. He seemed surprised since I never took a day off. I'm not sure what I was planning to do, but Alberto followed me downstairs and asked where I was going.

"I don't know," I told him.

Sensing that I was in trouble, he removed a piece of paper from his pocket and pressed it into my hand. "Please look at what I wrote and repeat this phrase when you're trying to decide what to do." We both knew what he was talking about.

I glanced at the paper: *Nam-myoho-renge-kyo.*

"It's a Buddhist phrase," he explained.

I glanced at the words again.

"It means that you dedicate your life to the law of cause and effect."

I shoved the note in my pocket.

"Trust me," he said, but I had a problem with that because it meant giving up control.

Still, while I shrugged him off, an idea seemed to be taking hold. Why not take the subway to the end of the line and get off at Coney Island? I wasn't sure what I'd do when I got there; I just knew I had to go.

When I came out of the station into the bright sunshine, I could feel the ocean breeze coming off the water. I had loved the ocean since my aunt Alice took me to Wildwood, New Jersey, when I was a teenager. Somehow being that close to the water seemed to clear my mind. On impulse I made my way to the New York Aquarium where I stopped to look at the penguins. I'd read that they have special adaptations that help them survive in their environment, like stiff flippers for flying in water and the ability to collect air in their feathers before going into the sea to provide insulation against the cold.

Watching them splash around in the dirty water and slip down the slides, I started to cry. They seemed so joyful. When three of them waddled over to take a good look at me, I felt an instant connection as if the little child in me had been reawakened. Removing the slip of paper from my pocket, I read the words aloud: *Nam-myoho-renge-kyo.*

     Brad Johns with Marianne Dougherty

What happened next was the first step in a spiritual journey that would lead me out of darkness into the light.

Later I'd learn that those words, from Sanskrit, were a pledge you made to yourself that you'd never yield to difficulties, that you would embrace your true Buddha nature. Repeating them over and over seemed to open a portal that allowed me to see everything from a different perspective. These magnificent creatures had not let their inability to fly impact their survival but had simply adapted to a life at sea where land predators wouldn't be a threat. They were in a pen at Coney Island, far from their natural habitat near the sea in Australia or Chile or South Africa, yet they seemed happy. I had everything, yet I wanted to end my life.

Suddenly, life seemed precious, and thoughts of suicide receded as I came to a powerful realization. I could think of myself as a victim or take responsibility for my life. That's the message I got from those penguins that day. Maybe if I made different choices from now on, better choices, I could change my life. Cause and effect. That day at the Aquarium felt like Easter, but I was keenly aware that I had paid a steep price for my resurrection: a descent into my own private hell.

13

Enlightenment is different for everyone. Siddhartha Gautama, the Buddha, received enlightenment under the Bodhi tree, a sacred fig at Bodh Gaya in Bihar, India. Mine came to me at the New York Aquarium, but it was powerful enough that I began studying Buddhism in earnest. I was no longer contemplating suicide, or at least it wasn't the first thing I thought about when I woke up.

My cousin Lynn, who was living in New York where she worked at CBS, joined me every day at the Zen Chogye International Center on 14th Street to say morning prayers with two or three hundred other people. You never knew who might show up. Tina Turner came on occasion. So did singer/songwriter Suzanne Vega, who became famous a few years later for songs like "Solitude Standing" and "Luka."

We practiced Nichiren Buddhism, which is based on the teachings of the thirteenth century Japanese Buddhist priest Nichiren. who established the practice of chanting *Nam-myoho-renge-kyo* to help us tap into our inherent Buddha nature.

The mantra itself means to dedicate your life to the law of cause and effect. *Nam* means dedication, while *myoho* means mystic or wonderful law, an expression of the dharma or underlying principal inherent in all life. *Renge* means lotus flower, which produces flowers and fruit at the same time, symbolizing the simultaneity of cause and effect. *Kyo* is the voice or teaching of the Buddha.

     Brad Johns with Marianne Dougherty

Chanting and meditation help you focus your concentration so you are better able to grasp the four noble truths. The first is suffering (*dukkha*). To suffer is to be alive. The second noble truth is *samydaya* or the root of suffering, which is attachment: to material possessions, to a particular outcome, to pleasure, which is fleeting. The third is *nirodha*, which offers the possibility of healing. *Magga*, the fourth noble truth, is the path to happiness: right views, right thought, right action, right livelihood, right effort, right mindfulness and right concentration.

I had felt like a victim for most of my life, but Buddhism changed my perspective. Understanding cause and effect taught me that the choices I make are what matter. Not my impoverished childhood. Not the bullies who tormented me. Not my inherent sadness. Gradually, I began to understand that happiness was not out of the question and that my life might be worth something.

The notion of cause and effect fascinated me, the idea that if you slap someone today, you'll probably get slapped by someone else, either literally or figuratively, tomorrow. The tide goes in and the tide goes out. I have always loved science, which is probably why I liked doing hair color. Mix certain chemicals in just the right way, and you'll get the results you want. *Cause and effect.* So, Buddhism made sense to me on some level. It was also a practice, not a religion, which appealed to me.

My parents didn't go to church for reasons I discovered much later, but my aunt Alice started taking me, Craig and Shari to mass with her and my cousins Lynn and Chris when I was still in grammar school. In a short, tight dress, stilettos clacking against the tile floor, Alice shepherded her little flock down the aisle to look for seats. When everyone turned to stare, I felt proud to be seen with this beautiful woman who looked nothing like the frumpy wives who glared at her. For a long time, I loved going to mass: the ritual, the papery communion wafers, the incense with its woody, almost spicy aroma.

Then in high school, a priest told me that I couldn't come to church wearing bell-bottom jeans. "I don't think Jesus cares what I wear to church," I told him.

"He might," the priest replied.

I never went to church again, but when I learned that my father wasn't permitted to go to mass because he had been married before he met my mother, I was done with religion. How had organized religion strayed so far from Jesus's teachings to become a source of power, greed and control? That's what I wanted to know.

Once I became a practicing Buddhist, I gave up drugs entirely. While it was a good decision for me, it alienated most of my friends, who were not inclined to follow my lead. Even now I remember feeling hurt and abandoned by everyone I used to party with as I sat by myself in my apartment on the first Saturday night of my new life.

What I've learned is that becoming is an alone process, something you have to do yourself. My friends simply weren't on my path yet. The charismatic Christian author Joyce Meyer says that when you invite God into your life, negative people won't want to be around you. It might feel like being in hell for a while, but the good news is that you'll live, you'll get through it.

Aside from my daily spiritual practice, I was also working out five days a week, two of them with a trainer. Over time I put on twenty pounds, which were all muscle. I'd given up alcohol as well, and I followed a macrobiotic diet to balance yin and yang: no meat, no dairy, lots of whole grains and seasonal vegetables and fruits.

I was very busy at the salon, but I was lonely. I had never looked better, yet I was afraid to be with anyone for fear of getting AIDS. I longed to kiss someone, missed the intimacy of being close to another person. Finally, I decided to go to Puerto Rico for a few days just to get away.

When I arrived, everything was boarded up in anticipation of a hurricane that was making its way toward the island. When the rain started coming down in sheets, I went to the beach where I almost got knocked over as the wind began to pick up. Hurricanes gather energy by breathing in warm, tropical air as they move across the ocean, then discharging cooler air into the atmosphere like a pair of lungs breathing in and out. The energy on the beach that day felt substantial and real, and it had a profound effect on me.

Thankfully, the hurricane passed over the island quickly and left no damage. The next day I went to the beach and stretched out on a towel in my Speedo. I noticed that a Puerto Rican kid was watching me, but instead of looking away, I held his gaze for a few moments. I had never been good at cruising, but I could tell he was interested so I started a conversation with him.

He seemed sweet, and when he suggested that we go somewhere where we could be alone, I agreed, though I was nervous at first. Here I was all alone in another country about to have sex (is that what we were going to do?) with a stranger who might be infected with HIV. Still, I was starved for affection so I took him back to my hotel. All we did that afternoon was kiss and touch each other as if trying to find a workaround for this awful disease, but the encounter had felt close to worship, and I felt hopeful about the future for the first time.

14

To celebrate the fact that I had decided not to end my life, Lynn threw a surprise birthday party for me at Splitz Café, a new champagne bar in the West Village. Since my birthday is only a few days before Halloween, Lynn was dressed like the Statue of Liberty.

She must have invited nearly a hundred people, and most of them showed up: Vivian and Robert, ex-boyfriends of mine, artists and fashion people, a few friends from Fire Island, some of the top teachers at the Buddhist center and hairdressers I'd worked with over the years, including my mentor, Don Matthews.

It was a humbling experience for me, and I was overcome with emotion. All these people were here to wish me a happy birthday, a birthday I had never planned on celebrating.

I know how many strings Lynn had to pull to get so many important people together at one time, but she is nothing if not tenacious. When she moved to New York, home to the biggest media conglomerates in the world, Lynn found work as a secretary at Wells Fargo, but her dream was to work in the entertainment industry. A head-hunter tailored her resume specifically for a job opening at CBS where she worked with casting directors and writers to develop new shows.

She likes to tell the story of how she worked as a temp for Walter Cronkite, who was writing his memoir. Mother's Day was coming up, and Alice adored him. What better Mother's Day gift than an autographed picture of the beloved news anchor? So, Lynn asked him to sign one of his headshots for her mother, and he was gracious enough to do it. In her office, Lynn burst out laughing when she examined the signature: *Walter "Lynn's Boss" Cronkite.* Apparently, Mr. C (that's what everyone at CBS called him) had a sense of humor.

Lynn could not wait for me to see the birthday cake she'd ordered for me. Written in icing were the words: *Glad you're alive in '85.* I lost it when I saw that cake. I don't even remember blowing the candles out or making a wish. Maybe my wish had already come true.

There were several TVs on the wall behind the bar, and I happened to notice that they were all tuned to the same station. The big story that month had been Rock Hudson's death on October 2 from AIDS, and reporters were still covering it. This was supposed to be a happy occasion, and the coverage felt ominous. Glancing around the restaurant, I was struck by the fact that half the people in this room might be dead in five years from the same disease, and I asked Lynn to change the channel. Jonathan and I were no longer together because he was unwilling to be monogamous, and I worried about him. What I didn't know at the time was that Don Matthews had already been diagnosed with HIV.

Don had come to Pittsburgh to meet my parents, and he sent a card to my mother right before he died: *It's time for me to go, but I'm going to pass the baton off to Brad.*

That's how much faith he had in me. I'm not sure I was ever able to fill his shoes, but I did my best.

15

ust like praying, chanting bolsters your intentions, and
my intention was to be the best colorist in the world,
a lofty pursuit but one that I was beginning to believe
was entirely within the realm of possibility. Buddhism not
only helped me set intentions but also develop the discipline
required to focus on what I wanted. Sometimes Lynn and I
would go to someone's apartment where we chanted *nam-myoho-renge-kyo* for two hours straight with a hundred
other people. When we were done, I felt like I was vibrating.
That's how powerful those sessions were.

For me, mediocrity is death. "If you're not good at
something," my father told me years before, "don't do it." I
knew I was a good colorist, but I also knew that I'd never
be satisfied unless I mastered my craft. While I had been
making good money at Clive Summers, I felt like it was time
to up my game so I applied for a job at Bruno Dessange.
The salon was a partnership between French hairdressing
legend Jacques Dessange, who had turned Brigitte Bardot
into a blonde for *And God Created Woman,* and his star hair
cutter, Bruno Pittini.

In its heyday, Bruno Dessange was a launching pad
for greatness if you were an ambitious and talented young
hairdresser. Frederic Fekkai and Yves Durif were rising stars
at Jacques Dessange in Paris when they were recruited to
work at Bruno Dessange in New York. Eventually, both of

them opened salons of their own. While Frederick's flagship salon on Fifth Avenue closed in 2018, Yves Durif is ensconced at the fabled Carlyle Hotel.

I knew that Bruno Dessange was *the* place to work when I scheduled an interview there. Buddhism had helped me to develop a strong sense of my worth as well as a "knowingness" when it came to making a career move that would be best for my art. So, while I had been making sixty percent commission at Clive Summers, I accepted Bruno Pittini's offer of forty percent, secure in the knowledge that I was on the right path. Within a year, I was promoted from colorist to color director.

There was only one catch. I'd be required to do balayage, a highlighting technique developed in Paris. Instead of using foils, color was applied directly onto the hair in broad, sweeping strokes. In theory, balayage creates sun-kissed color that requires less upkeep as it grows out, but in my experience the high concentrations of peroxide damage the hair.

I had been experimenting with a new technique that would allow me to create light and warmth around the face by applying bleach directly to big sections of hair. Timing was critical; the trick was not to leave the bleach on too long, maybe a minute or two, maybe less. The idea came to me after I remembered watching my mother and her friends dip a toothbrush into a cup of peroxide and apply it to a big chunk of dark hair right up front. The results were nothing like the buttery blonde shade I was after since they had no idea how to lift hair past the tacky orange stage, but they had what I called the "oomph factor."

Meanwhile, I had been hearing a lot about a hairdresser named Oribe whose work—big hair inspired by girls he knew growing up in North Carolina—was being featured on the covers of fashion magazines. There were rumors that his boyfriend, booker and manager had negotiated a deal with Elizabeth Arden for a salon on the tenth floor that would not only invigorate the brand but also be the crown jewel atop the iconic building on Fifth Avenue. Omar was a shrewd businessman, and when he and Oribe walked into a club like the Sound Factory dressed in Chrome Hearts leather and motorcycle boots, everyone turned to stare because they were so breathtaking.

Born in Jaruco, Cuba, in 1956, Oribe was six years old when his family moved to Charlotte, North Carolina. With dreams of becoming an actor, he moved to New York City when he was eighteen and found work serving salad and dessert at a club called the Blue Angel. "It was French and had dancers," is how he remembered it. When the club burned down, he got a job as a receptionist at a friend's salon on Third Avenue and decided to go to beauty school. Someone introduced him to Garren, who was opening a salon at the Plaza Hotel. Already a well-known editorial hairdresser with a celebrity clientele that included Brooke Shields and Farrah Fawcett, he hired Oribe to be his assistant.

From there he went to work at the Private World of Leslie Blanchard, a high-end salon on 62nd Street. Blanchard was a world-famous hairdresser who had appeared in ads for Clairol in the 1960s and had a stable of celebrity clients like Meryl Streep and Cathy Moriarity (he bleached her hair white for *Raging Bull*). It was there that Oribe learned a lot about hair color and had his first brush with celebrity, admitting that since he was so much younger than anyone else, he got to work with all the cool movie stars.

     Brad Johns with Marianne Dougherty

When Garren hired him back, Oribe got his first big break when he was asked to style a story for *GQ*, and doors began to open for him—work with the French stylist, art director and photographer Carlyn Cerf, who had resigned from *Elle* in France to become the editorial director of the Conde Nast group; a long run with photographer Richard Avedon, who had been hired to make over *Self* magazine.

Then he got a call from a new photographer named Steven Meisel, who was getting a lot of work for *Mademoiselle*. For the next seven years, Oribe worked with Meisel and makeup artist Francois Nars on fashion spreads for *Vogue*, *Harper's Bazaar* and *W*, describing their collaboration as magical.

Big hair was Oribe's stock in trade, and he excelled at creating towering confections for models like Cindy Crawford, Christy Turlington and Linda Evangelista, almost single-handedly inventing the supermodel. There would be no J Lo without Oribe, who styled her hair for her debut album, *On the 6*. Later, he told a reporter for *The New York Times* that Jennifer Lopez was "a big-hair kind of girl." The two of them became fast friends, traveling all over the world together, she and Oribe in one plane, her wardrobe following behind in another. That was the '90s for you, an era of over-the-top excess in every way.

I regarded Oribe as a kindred spirit, someone who was able to take something that others might find in bad taste and make it respectable. I always said that Oribe did for hairdressing what Arnold Schwarzenegger did for bodybuilding. In his hands, hair became an art form. I was trying to do the same thing with hair color.

When Oribe invited me to have dinner with him and Omar, I had no idea that he'd ask me to be color director at his new salon. While I knew it was the chance of a lifetime, I also had reservations. The way most colorists highlighted hair in those days was with a frosting cap. It was a painful process for the client because it required you to pull hair through holes in a plastic cap at random with a crochet hook. Results were haphazard at best, and the color looked ashy. I was convinced that women look better in warm, golden shades, but I also hated the fact that you ended up with tiny little highlights, which I abhorred. I didn't like doing balayage at Bruno Dessange, and I certainly had no desire to do frostings either, but what if that's what Oribe wanted?

As it turned out, Oribe hated frostings as much as I did. When he told me he thought hair color should look artistic, I knew we had the same aesthetic. For me, hair color is an art form, and I was working on a technique that delivered results not unlike the paintings of Picasso or Ellsworth Kelly: big, bold and brash.

Oribe came up with the name "chunking" to describe my technique for highlighting hair with more precision, placing lighter pieces in big chunks around the face so it resembled the way a child's hair looked after a summer at the beach. I accepted Oribe's offer that night, and our collaboration over the next five years elevated my career to a whole new level.

In 1991, work began on Oribe's $3 million salon, which he imagined as an Italian whorehouse from the 1920s: Venetian chandeliers overhead to reflect the light, antique mirrors, ornate furnishings, everything very glam and very gold with burgundy accents. He would cut hair in a rotunda with a mirrored ceiling, six gold chairs with burgundy upholstery and Venetian-style paintings on the walls.

     Brad Johns with Marianne Dougherty

He let me design the color room to my specifications: six mirrors, six chairs, two sinks on one side and two on the other and a dispensary to store the supplies we'd need to formulate color. I just assumed he knew that the walls had to be white. Artists paint in studios with stark-white walls, art galleries display paintings on stark-white walls, but stark-white walls in his gilded palace were not what Oribe had in mind. His instructions were that the color room be painted gold like everything else.

When I told him he'd have to repaint, he almost had a heart attack. He's just spent a fortune to use gold leaf on the walls, and here I was telling him that it had to go. I explained that all that gold paint would reflect too much gold in the hair color once I'd finished and that I wouldn't be able to see the true results.

"I'll have to take my clients outside just to see if the color is right," I told him, which both of us knew was unfeasible. We fought back and forth for days, but finally we reached a compromise and agreed on a pearly shade of white that seemed to satisfy his need for glitz.

To celebrate the grand opening of the salon, Oribe threw an elaborate party that attracted so much press it resembled a movie premiere. Editors mingled with models and actresses, most of them wearing leopard prints, which were big then. Dressed in a gold snakeskin bikini and see-through top, Swedish model and actress Vendela was carried in on a litter by a team of bodybuilders like she was Cleopatra. The drinks were flowing, and there was lots of Italian food. Oribe may have been Cuban, but he loved everything about Italy, which for him was synonymous with art, architecture and painting.

I wore a silver snakeskin tank, skintight black leather pants, multiple silver bracelets I'd made myself and high-heeled shoes from Ian's, the boutique on St. Mark's Place where all the rock stars shopped. That night my shoulder-length hair was dark brown, my natural color, but after chunking took off, I became lighter and brighter. I wanted clients to know that anyone could be a blonde even if they had hair as dark as mine.

My staff followed suit, and we all became walking bill-boards for the kind of results we were able to achieve in the salon. Rita Hazan, who has become a celebrity colorist in her own right, was one of my assistants. Her hair is as dark as mine so we had to touch up her roots every week. I had an Asian assistant named Adrian whose hair was almost black, but I was able to lift his hair to a shade of flaxen blonde without damage because I knew how to use Clairol products to produce the results I wanted.

Oribe's salon was a breeding ground for talent. Serge Normant, one of the leading editorial stylists in the world, worked there. So did Francois Nars and makeup artist Laura Mercier. Never one to micromanage anyone, Oribe fed his famous clients to us and let us do our thing. He introduced me to Carolyn Bessette when she was working at Calvin Klein and had yet to meet her future husband, John F. Kennedy, Jr.

Like I've said before, the power of intention is strong. My intention was to be the best hair colorist in the world, and making the move from Bruno Dessange to work with Oribe was my intention writ large. I had dreamed this, and now it was real.

16

The New Age Health Spa sits on two hundred and eighty acres in Neversink, New York, deep in the Catskills. Originally, the place was known as a "fat farm" when it was purchased by Werner Mendel, who made his money on Wall Street, and his wife, Canadian social worker Stephanie Paradise. They transformed it into a destination spa, though one that looked less like Canyon Ranch and more like a dude ranch. The rooms were spartan, and there were no telephones or televisions in any of them.

I knew that Shari and my mother wanted to lose a few pounds so I booked rooms for them at the resort. My mother was a heavy smoker at the time, but she also had a sweet tooth. Unfortunately for her, tobacco and sugar were strictly verboten at the New Age Health Spa. At the entrance, a sign hammered into a post above a trash barrel admonished you to "leave your worries, cigarettes, candy, alcohol and drugs here." They meant business, and the trash barrel was emptied daily.

They had been there for a week when I joined them for a four-day juice fast and colonics. Unable to indulge her craving for sweets, my mother was not a happy camper. Like a junkie jonesing for heroin, she needed a fix, and what she wanted was a doughnut. I had to make some excuse about going into town to fill a prescription so we could leave the property. Finding a doughnut shop in the middle of nowhere took some effort, but we did.

When we got back to her room, I discovered a carton of contraband Benson & Hedges she had not tossed into the trash barrel. To her credit, she hadn't smoked a single cigarette. By the end of her stay, my mother might not have lost any weight, but she did quit smoking cold turkey, which is something I suppose.

Our days were filled with yoga, dance, meditation, Tai Chi and other activities, but occasionally there were programs in the evening designed to inform or enlighten. It was my mother who talked us into seeing a spiritual teacher and author named J.Z. Knight who claimed to channel the spirit of a 35,000-year-old entity named Ramtha the Enlightened One.

My mother had a built-in bullshit detector; she just knew when someone was faking it or downright lying. She also hated blondes, and J.Z. Knight was a blonde. I've always suspected that my mother wanted to see for herself if J.Z. Knight was a charlatan.

Ramtha's teachings follow the gnostic tradition in which humans are divine entities who came from the spiritual realm but are trapped in this world. That message—that human beings have the capacity to utilize their inner wisdom, focus their brains and create their own reality—resonated with me, and I ordered dozens of Ramtha tapes on VHS. I was living an austere life at the time: up at five a.m. to meditate before working out at the gym, see clients all day, go home and watch a Ramtha tape before going to sleep. Living a life that clean may be what saved me when so many of my friends were dying of AIDS.

J.Z. Knight was not without detractors. Shirley McClain, an early devotee, broke off contact with Knight more than thirty years ago, and skeptics have pointed out that Knight

     Brad Johns with Marianne Dougherty

has become a millionaire since opening Ramtha's School of Enlightenment in Yelm, Washington, in 1988. She was also accused of being a fraud who faked Ramtha's appearances, though a series of psychological tests administered in 1997 suggested that her trance state was genuine and not symptomatic of any underlying mental illness.

The fact remains that I was deeply moved by Ramtha's message—that God is not a remote entity but part of everything in the universe and that consciousness and energy create the nature of reality. Perhaps it was the message, not the messenger, that was important, and that message resonated with me when I desperately needed it.

My personal path to enlightenment has taken a circuitous course, from Buddhism to Ramtha to Zoroastrianism, which is based on the teachings of the Iranian-speaking prophet Zoroaster and predicts that good will ultimately triumph over evil. One thing that's remained constant is that God has always told me when it's time to move on, and I have usually heard his voice when a prophet begins to profit from the ideology they're espousing.

I had become disenchanted with Buddhism when one of the elders at Zen Chogye International Center told me that I could not use a set of crystal and silver mala beads I'd made in jewelry class. He offered no further explanation, but I was reminded of the priest who told me that I couldn't wear blue jeans to mass. Later I was summoned to the office of someone with a lot more authority than the elders, who told me that they were worried that I might start selling my beads to other devotees. I assured him that I was not interested in making any more beads to sell and that I had made this set for myself in order to honor the Gohonzon, which is a scroll containing Chinese and Sanskrit characters that helps practitioners of Nichiren Buddhism to bring forth the life condition of Buddhahood.

He was quiet for a moment, and then he asked if I'd trade my beads for his set of wooden mala beads. I guess that was the turning point for me, and I told him that I would not be coming back.

The British historian Lord Acton famously said, "Absolute power corrupts absolutely." Add money to the equation and see what happens. To encourage parishioners to give generously, the Catholic church I attended until I was a teenager published a list of donations by family each year. The shame of seeing our name, Johns, next to a zero remained with me for years.

Richard Rohr is an American Franciscan priest and writer on spirituality based in Albuquerque, New Mexico. On his podcast "Another Name for Every Thing," he discussed the Jesus movement and how its message has become diluted over time. Tracing the movement of Christianity from its earliest days until now, he said, "In Israel, Jesus and the early 'church' offered people an experience; it moved to Greece, and it became a philosophy. When it moved to Rome and Constantinople, it became organized religion. Then it spread to Europe, and it became a culture. Finally, it moved to North America and became a business."

When faith or religion or the church becomes a business, I want no part of it. What I longed for was what Rohr calls the "Jesus experience," but it took me nearly thirty years to find it. Like I said, my path to enlightenment has been a circuitous one.

     Brad Johns with Marianne Dougherty

The past beats inside me like a second heart.

—JOHN BANVILLE, *THE SEA*

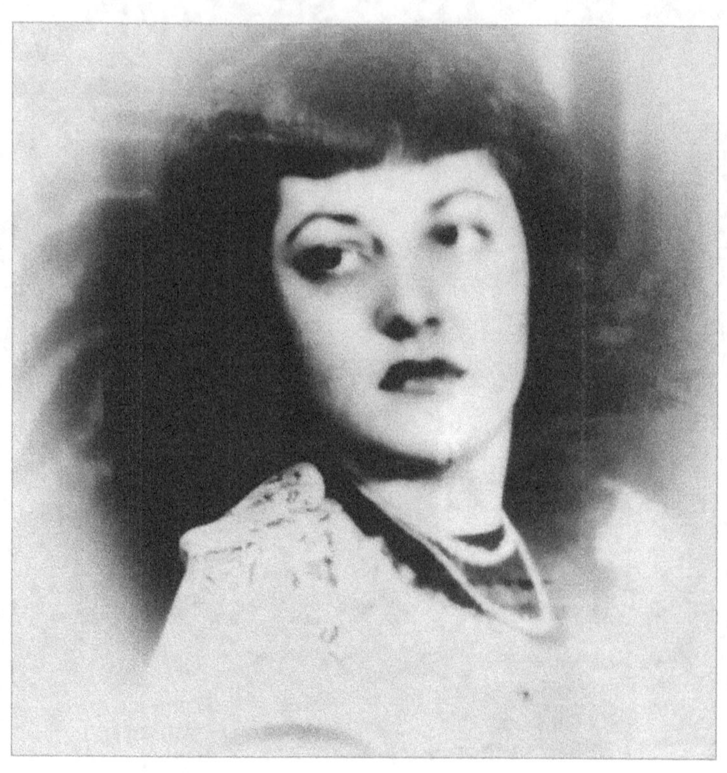

My mother, Thelma Rose Ciccone, at 18

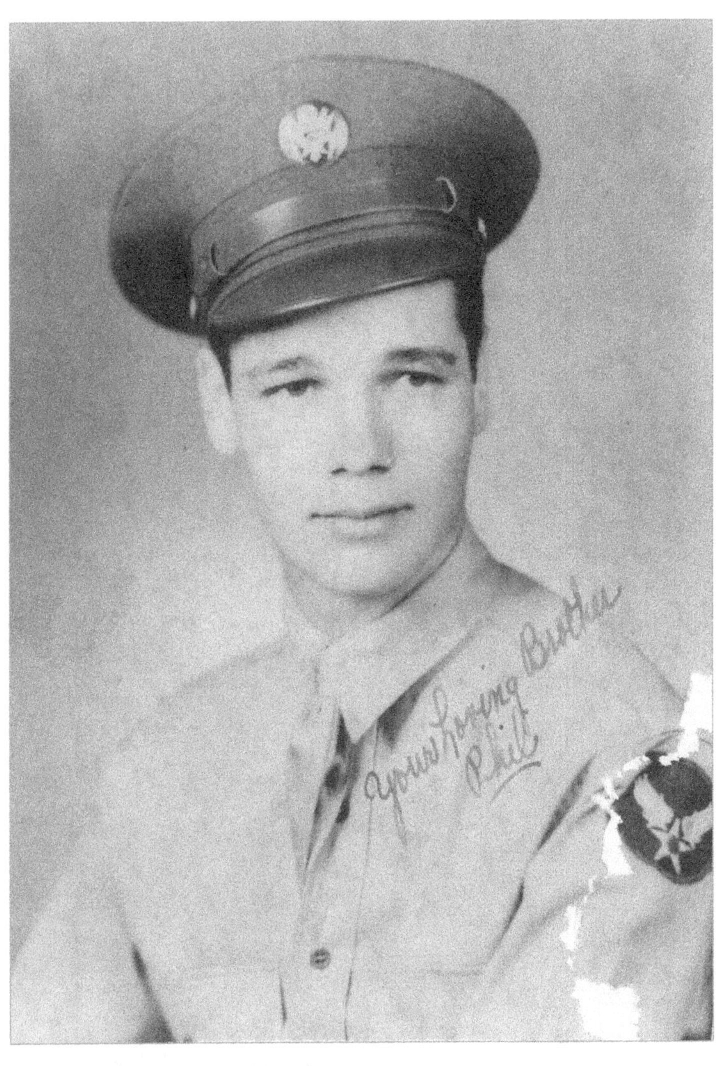

My father, Phillip Carlton Johns, in his Air Force uniform

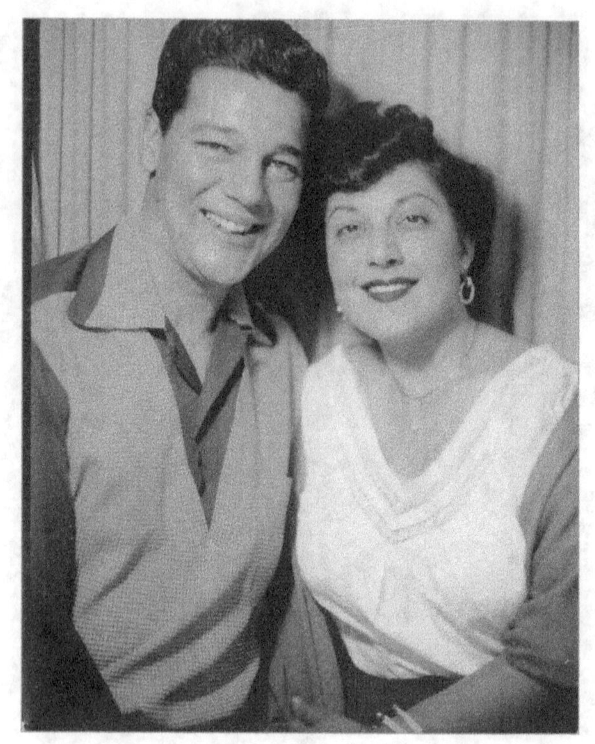

My glamorous parents early in their marriage

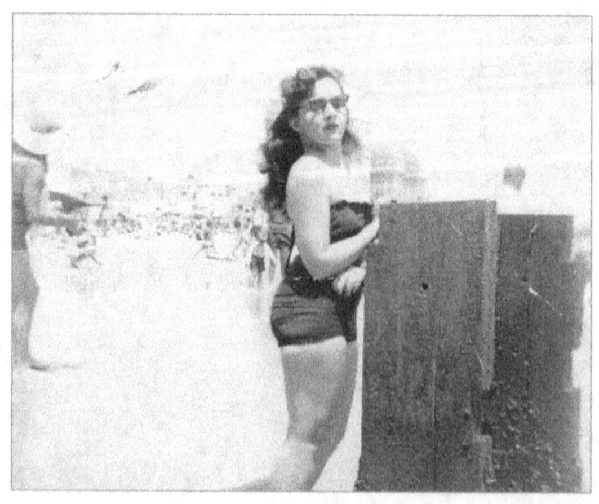

My beautiful aunt Alice at the Jersey Shore

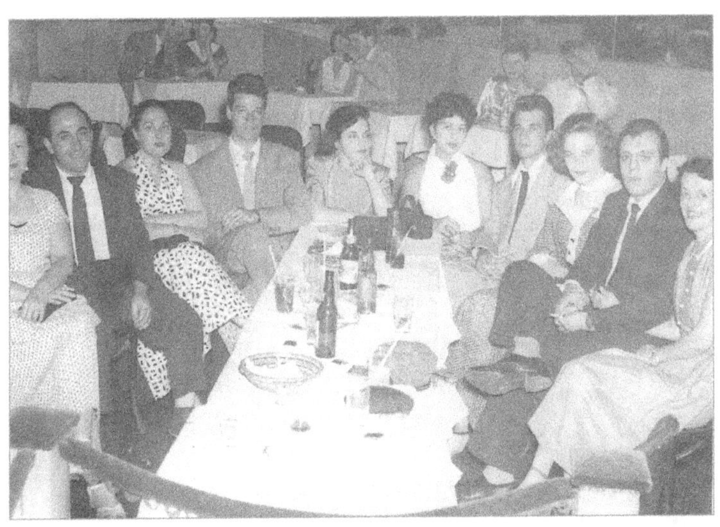

My father (center) with my mother on his right and my aunt Alice on his left at Lenny Litman's Copa in downtown Pittsburgh where they went to have dinner and listen to live jazz with family and friends In the 1950s

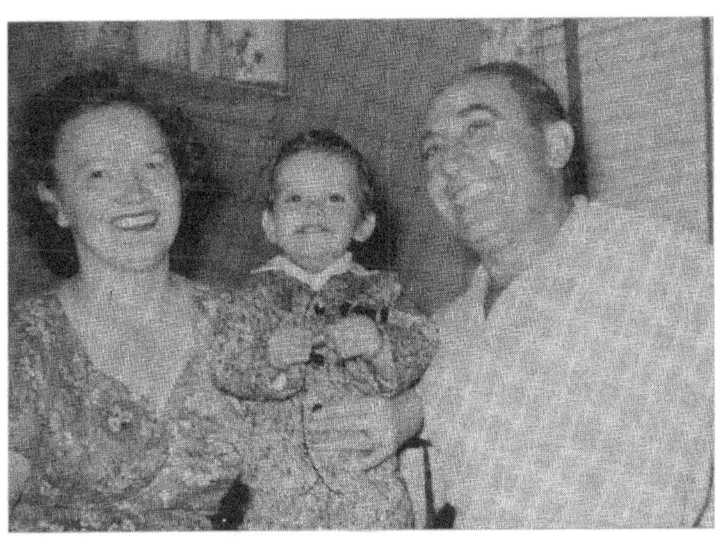

On Easter Sunday with my maternal grandparents, Grace and Salvatore Ciccone, during happier times

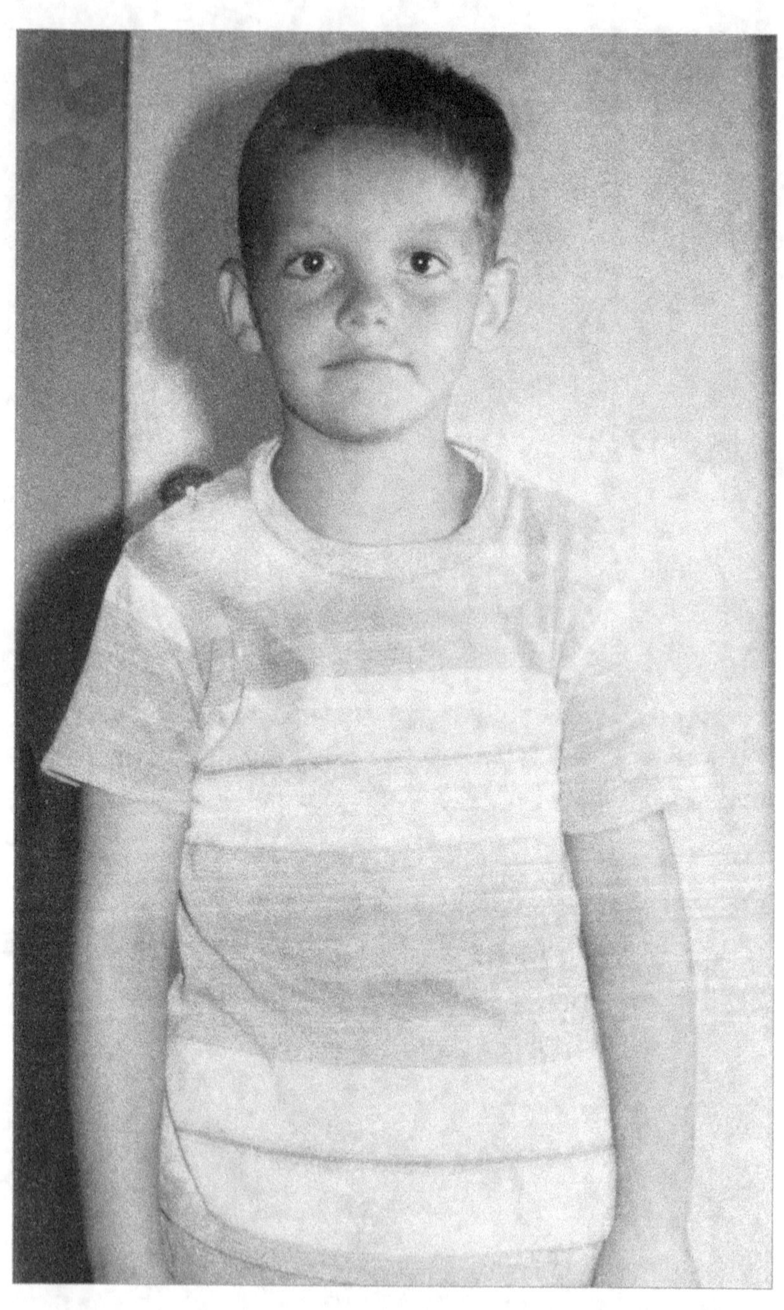

When I think of my inner child, who I call Little B, he looks like I did at six years old

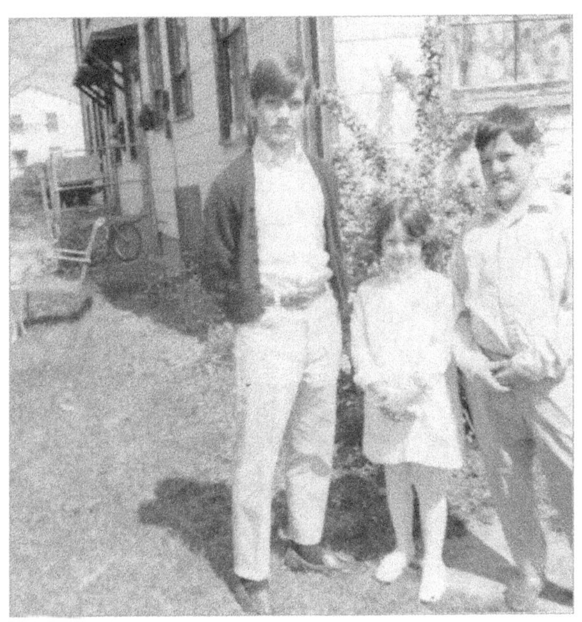

With my sister Shari and my brother Craig at OVA, probably the last time I wore khakis and loafers

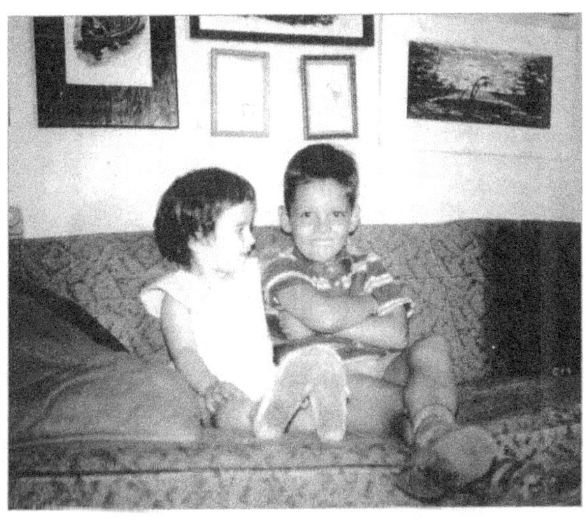

At our grandmother's house where I'm perfecting my bossy look as my cousin Lynn looks on adoringly

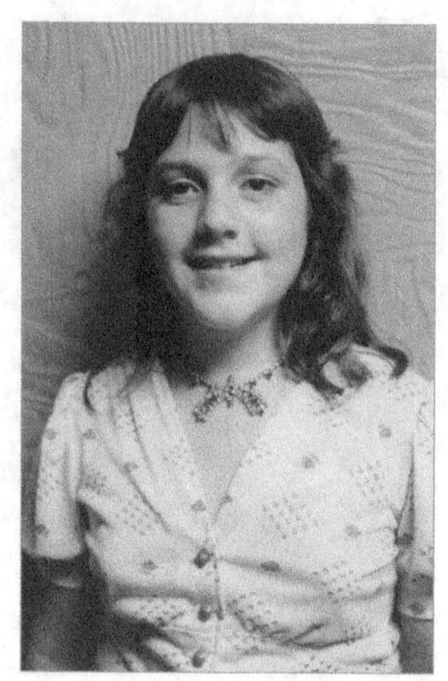

My sister Shari age 12

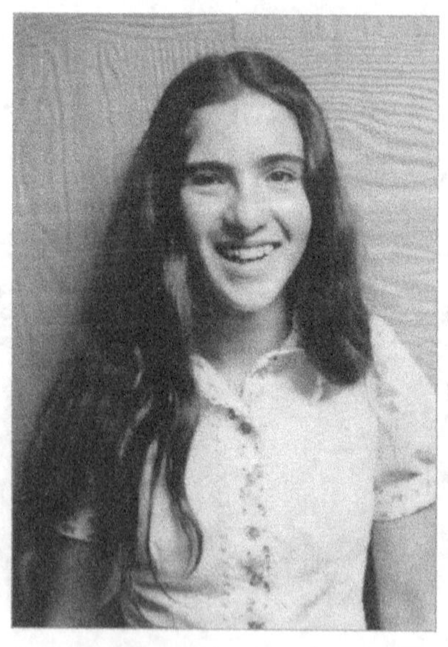

My cousin Lynn age 14

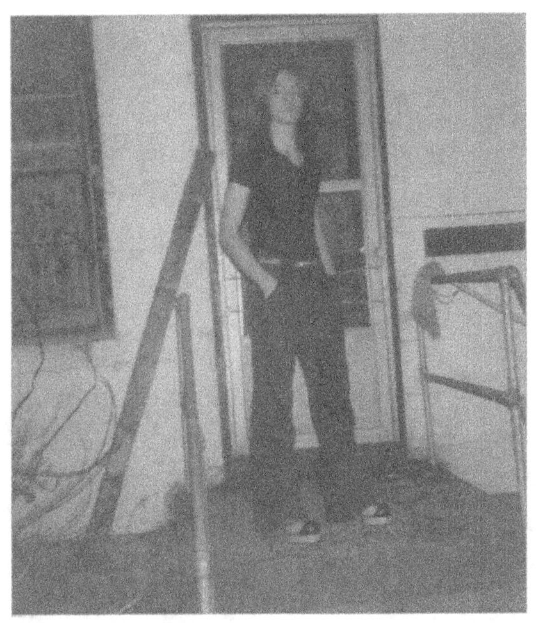

*In my powder-blue platform shoes on our front porch at OVA the day
I left for New York to audition at Stella Adler*

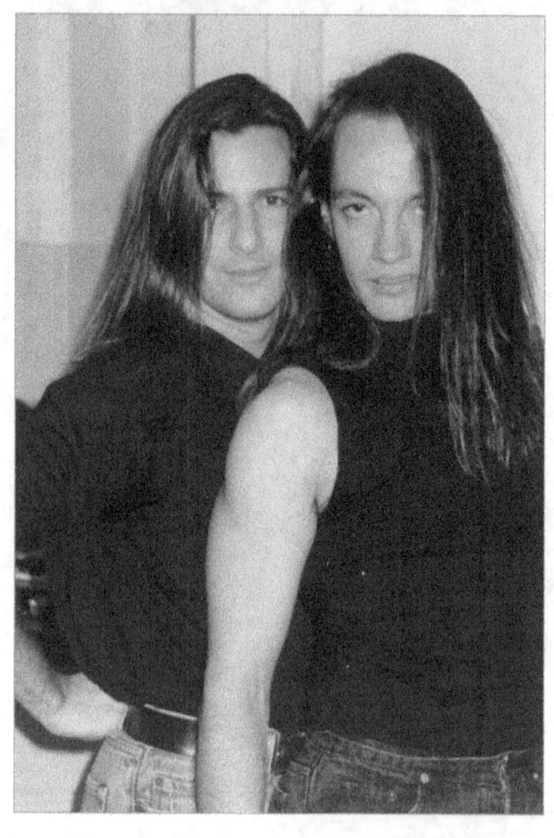

Chris and I dressed for the Roxy, the finest roller-disco in New York City in the 1970s

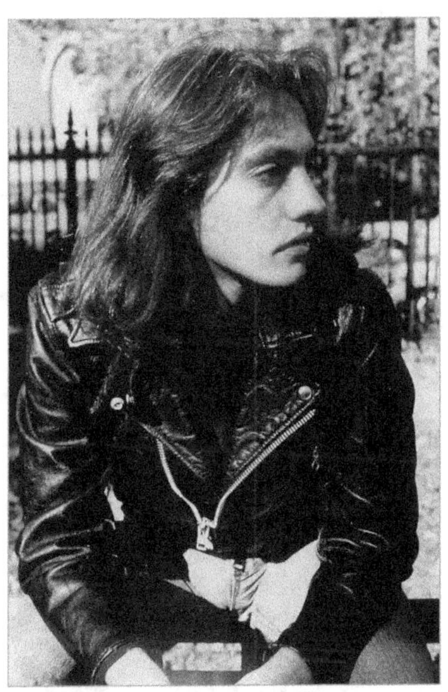

*In long hair and my leather motorcycle jacket at
Stuyvesant Square Park in New York*

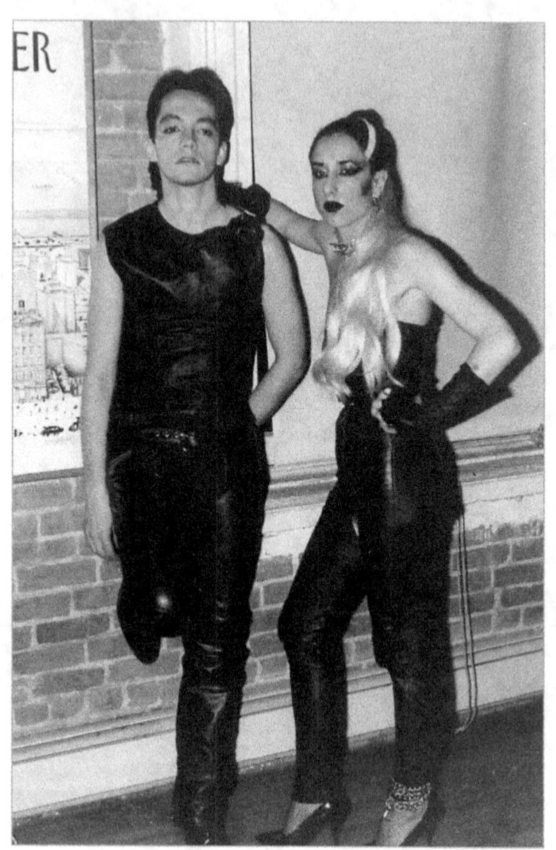

With Vivian on our way to the Mudd Club circa 1980

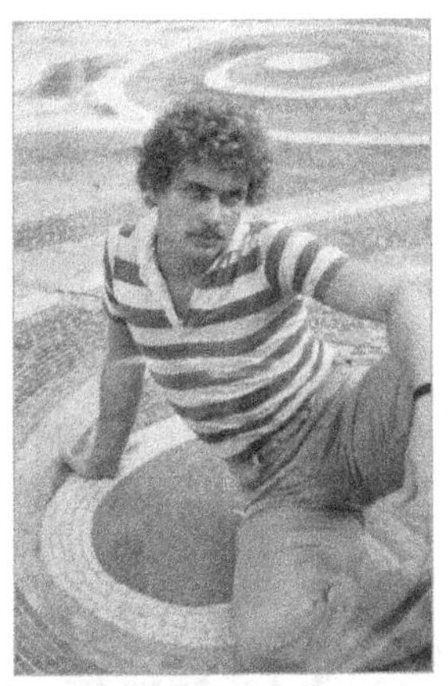

Raul was the love of my life.

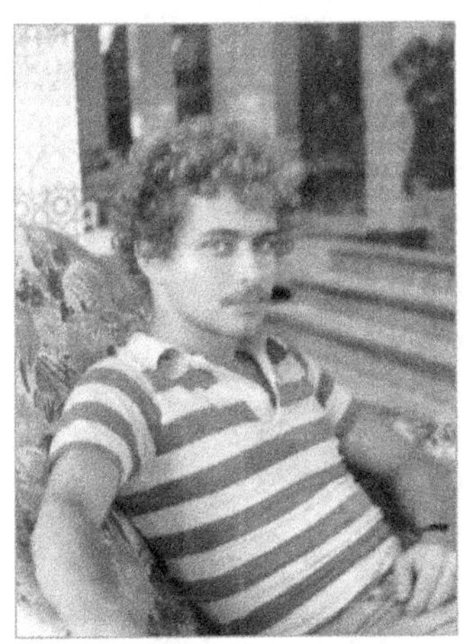

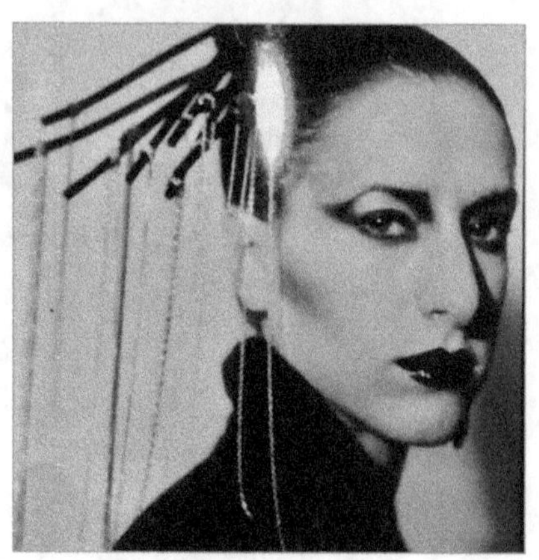

*Vivian let Raul and I do her hair and makeup for a test,
and I made hair jewelry out of chopsticks and silver chains.*

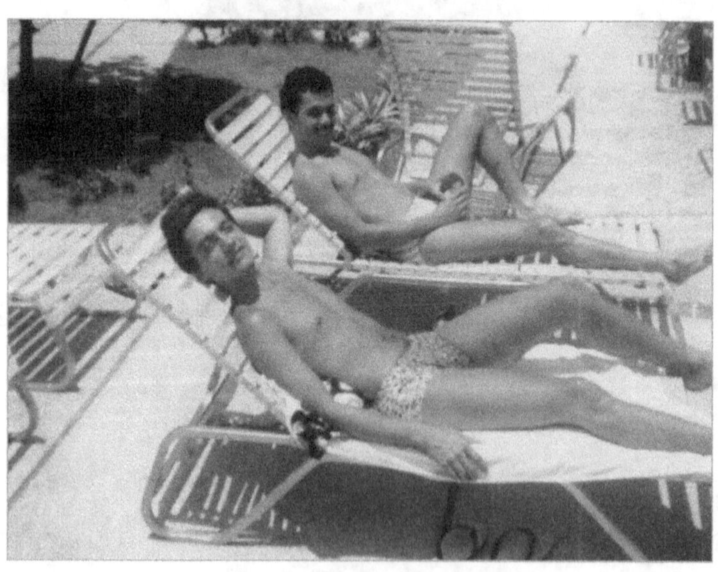

*Slim, tan and high in my Norma Kamali bikini
with a friend in Puerto Rico*

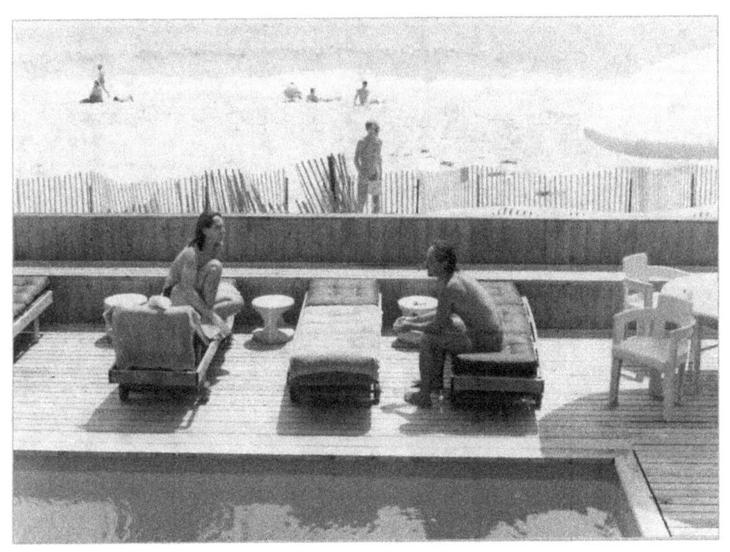

Soaking up the sun on Fire Island

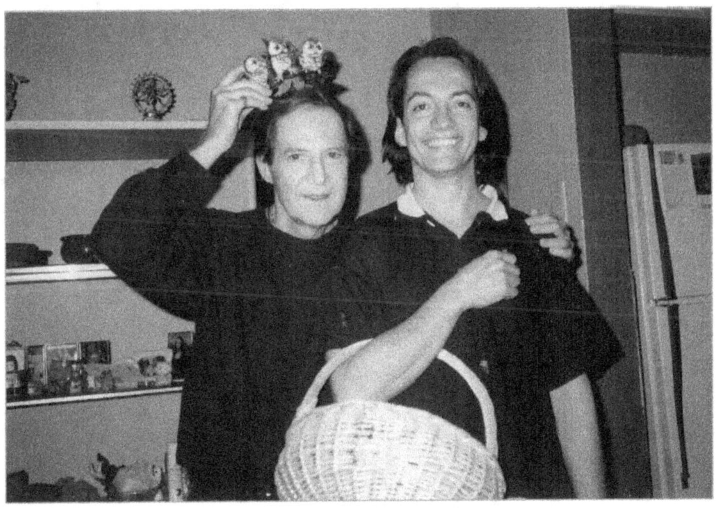

*With my mentor Don Matthews at my
mother's house in Pillsburgh*

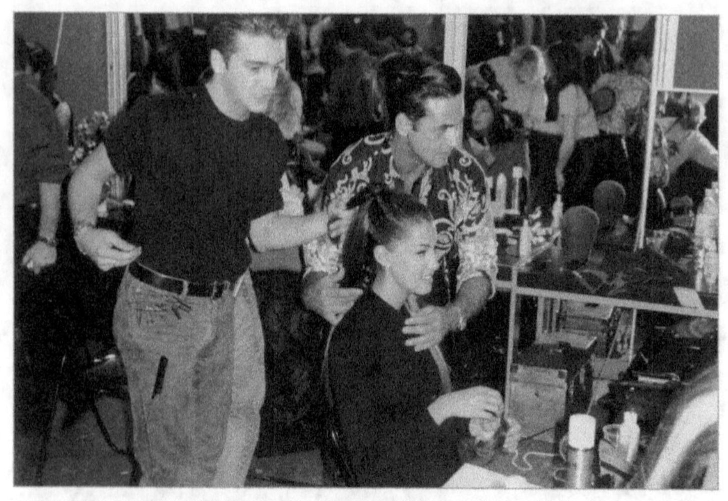

Oribe backstage at Versace in one of the designer's shirts

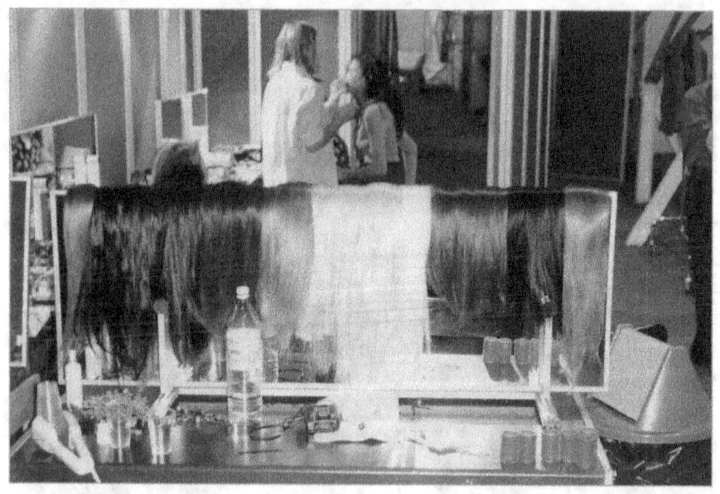

*Hairpieces I dyed for Oribe to use for Versace's
show at fashion week in Milan*

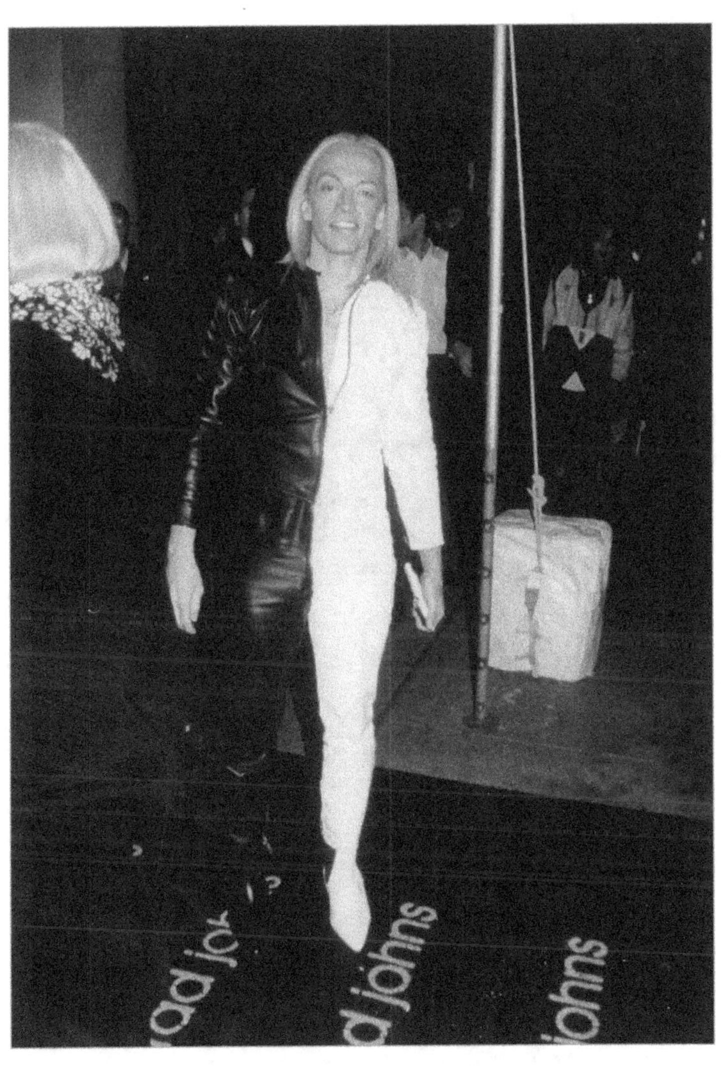

*The custom-made leather jumpsuit I wore to the opening
of my salon where the décor was black and white*

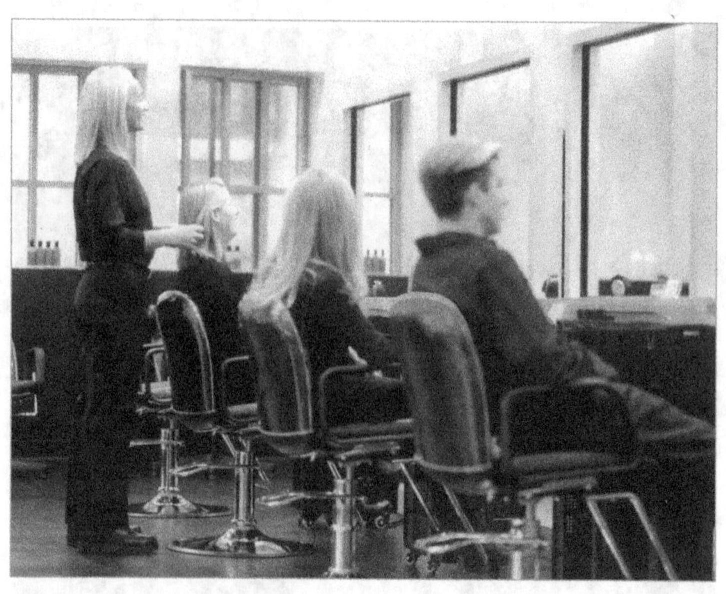

*In my element at my own salon in the days when I was
called the "golden boy" and the "color czar"*

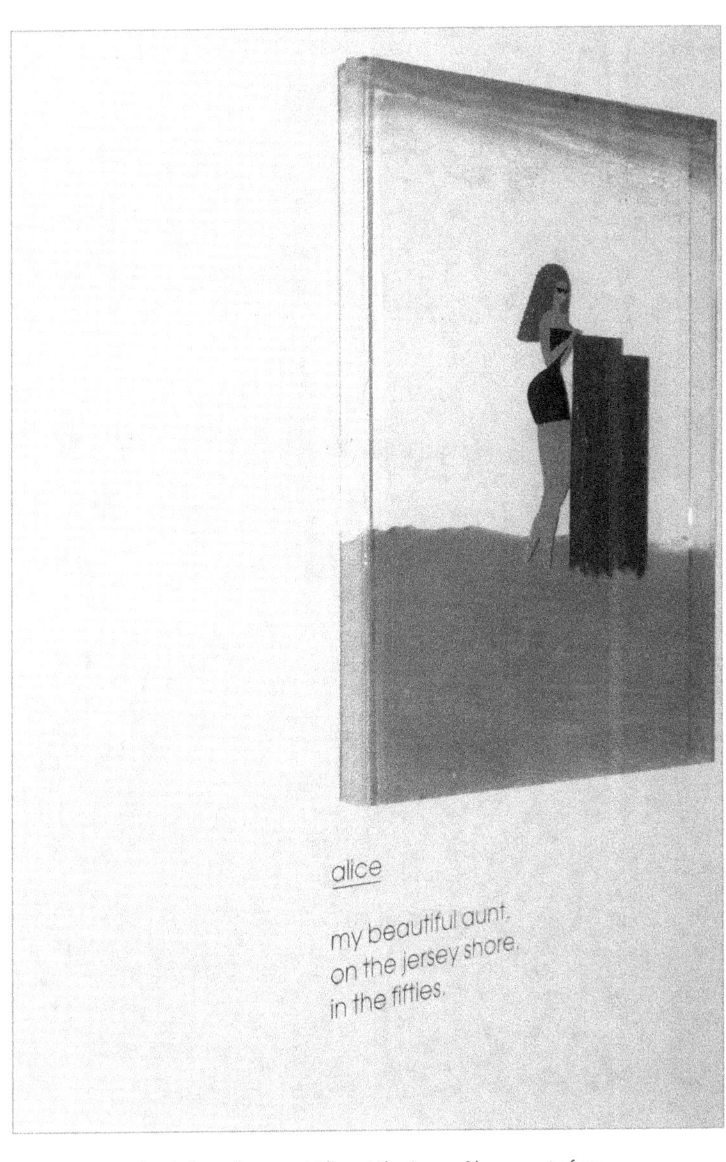

*A painting of my aunt Alice at the Jersey Shore, part of my
Anodyne Collection, which was shown at a gallery in Chelsea*

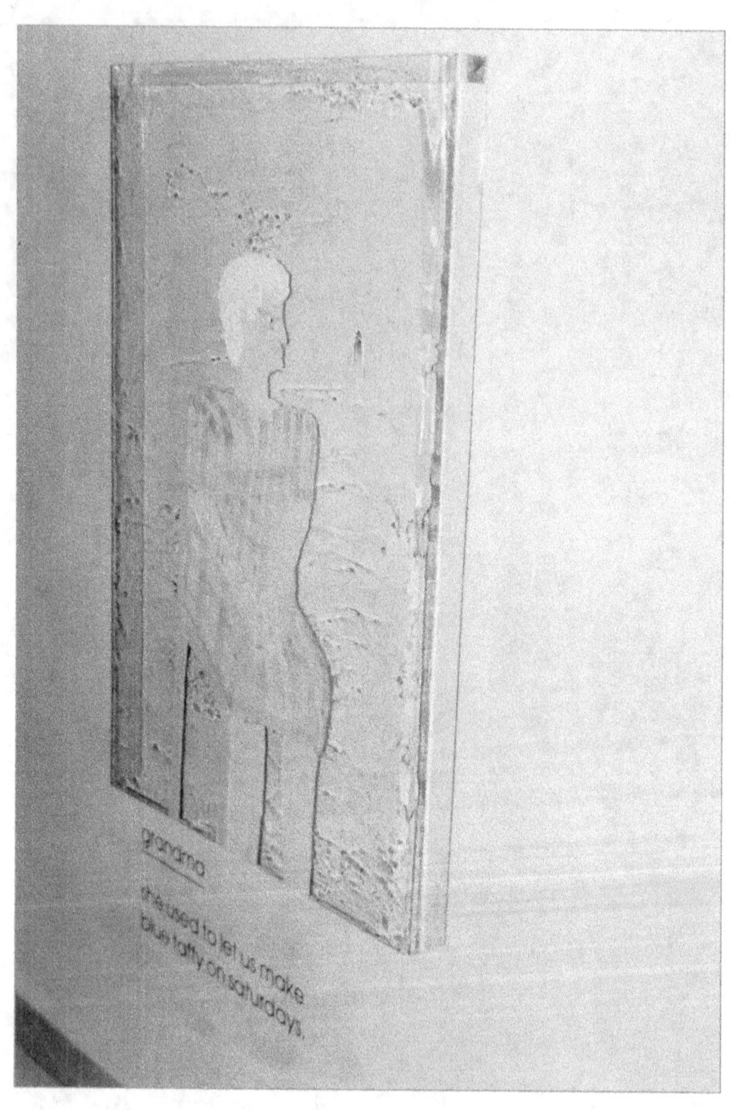

*A painting of my beloved grandmother, also part
of the Anodyne Collection*

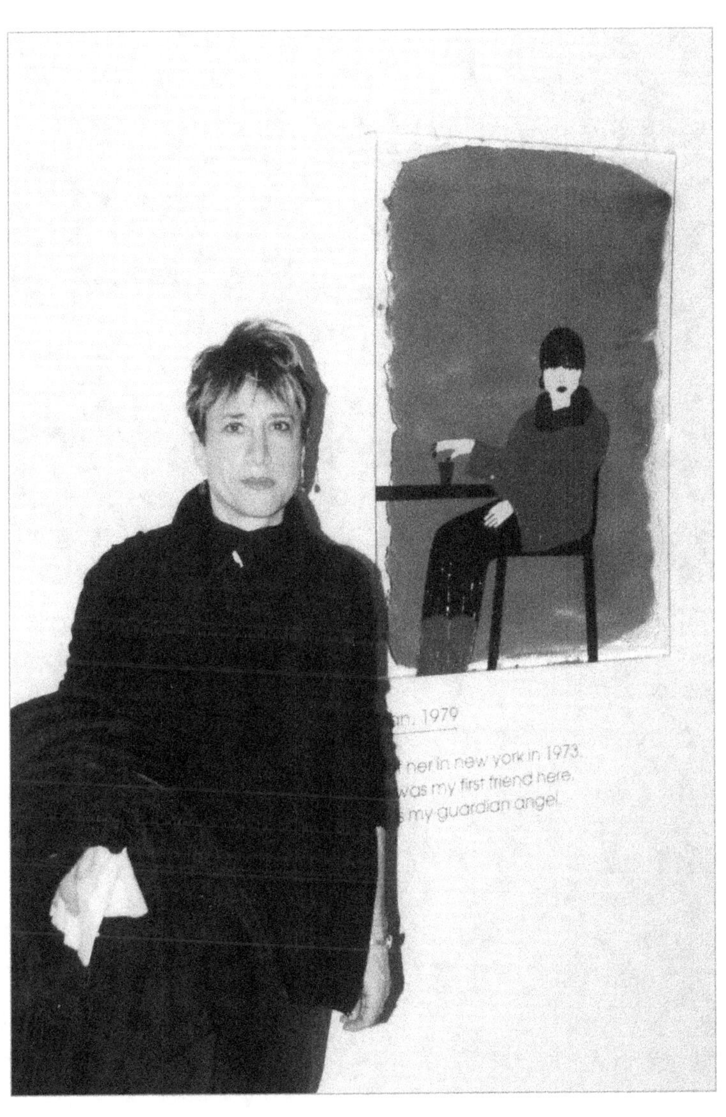

*Vivian next to the painting of her that was
part of the Anodyne Collection*

VIPs got this invitation from Avon to "Curtains," an exhibit of my paintings with proceeds earmarked for cancer research.

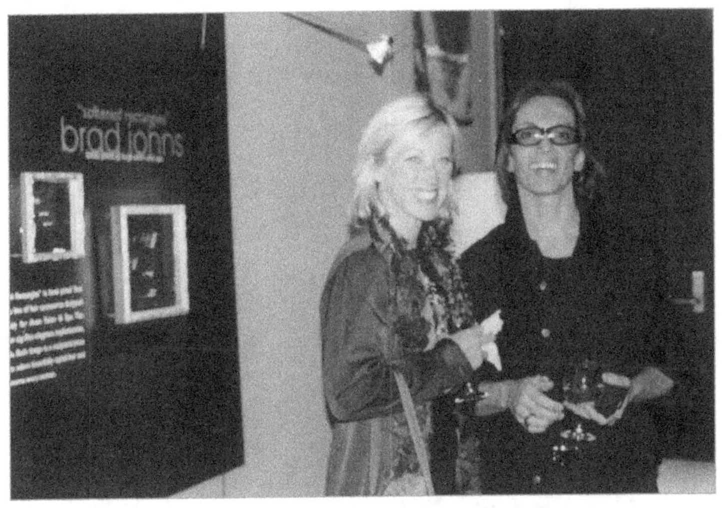

*Cindy Sherman came to see "Curtains" at Avon where
my silver hair jewelry was on display.*

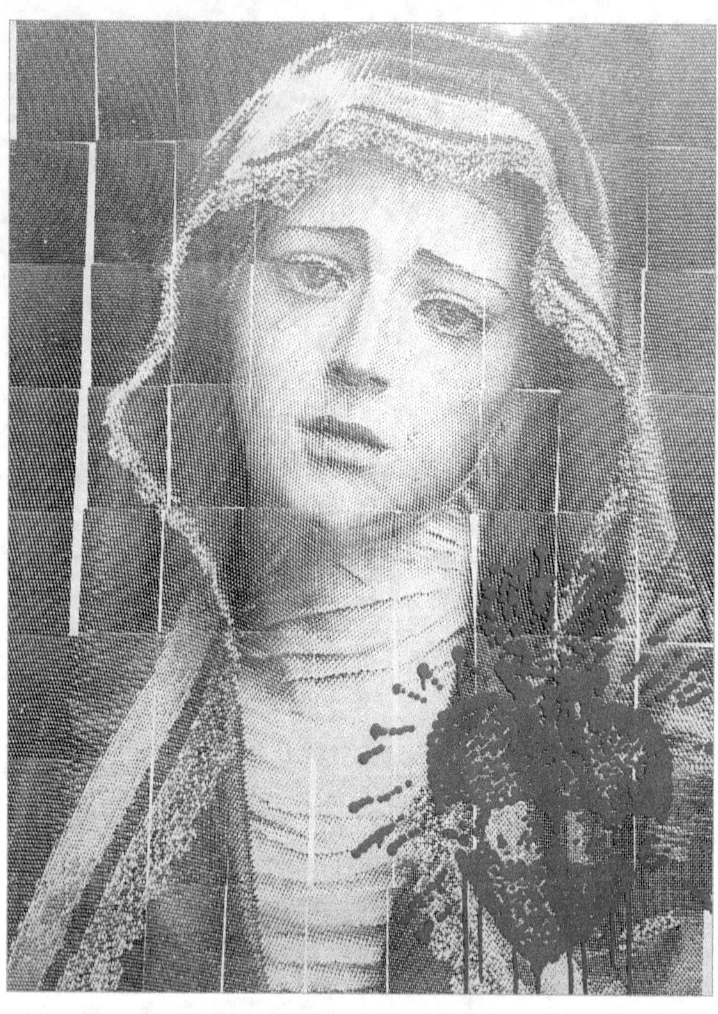

*The church my aunt Alice took me to as a child was called Mother of Sorrows so when I discovered a piece by artist Conner Meagher called **The Mother of Sorrows** (thermal labels, acrylic paint on repurposed frame) at Allgorithim on Melrose Avenue in West Hollywood, I had to have it.*

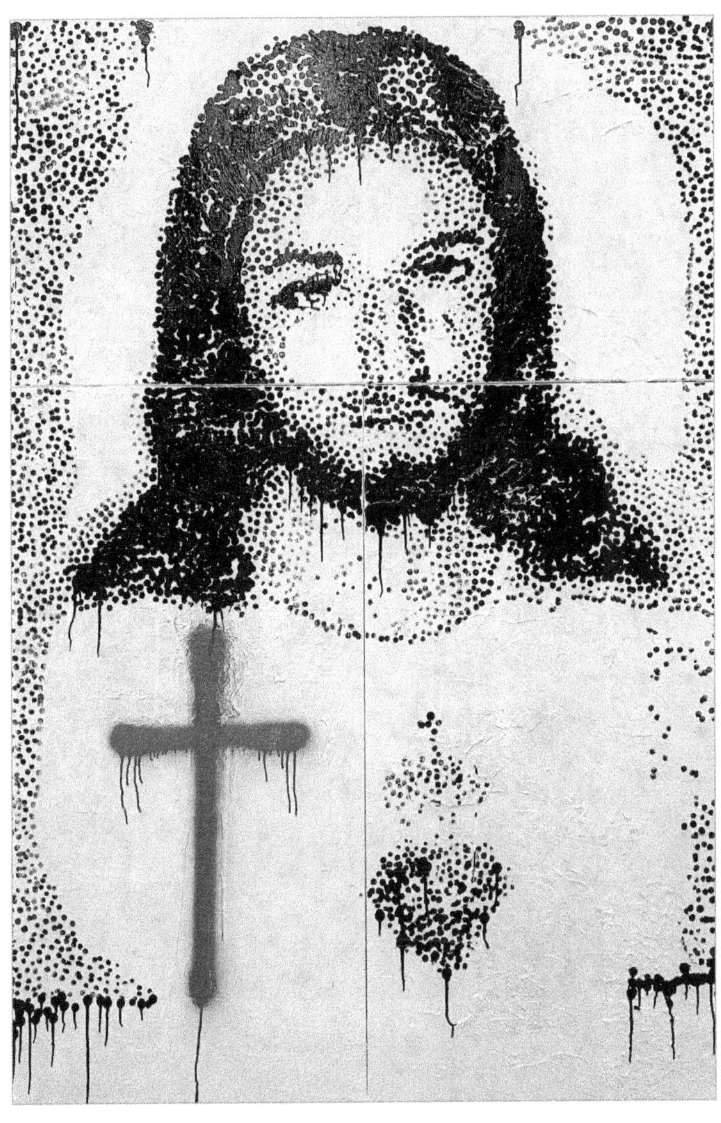

The Man of Man (eggshell paint/primer, spray paint and alcohol paint on canvas) is the second piece by Conner Meagher that I bought for obvious reasons.

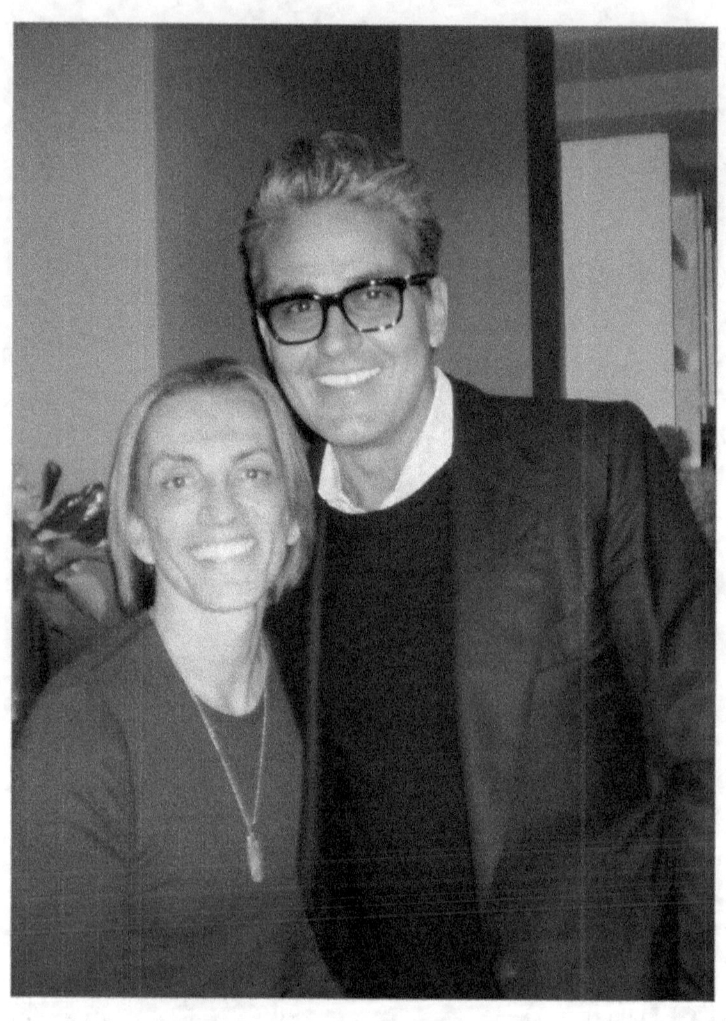

Artistically, Oribe and I were kindred spirits.

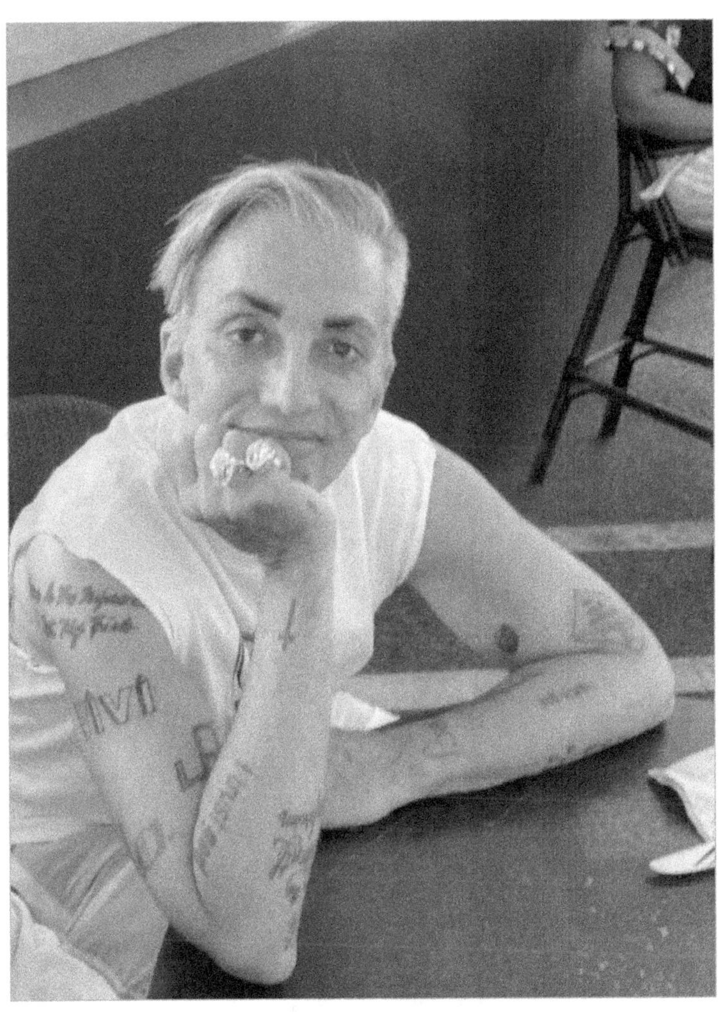

My tattoos tell a story, and each of them is very personal to me.

17

ll the supermodels came to Oribe to have their hair done, but my favorite was Christy Turlington. Ours was not just a professional relationship; we became close friends. Christy had never colored her hair, which was light brown. For a colorist, a head of virgin hair is a dream come true: a clean canvas upon which to create your art. I had already told Oribe I wasn't ready to try my chunking technique on any models yet since I was still trying to work out the kinks. The chunks were either too big or too white, or something else was off.

One afternoon when the receptionist told me that one of my clients had canceled her appointment, which rarely happened, I decided to go outside and get some fresh air. I took the elevator to the first floor and pushed through Elizabeth Arden's iconic red door, and there was Christy twirling for a photographer in a short floral-print dress. She looked like a fawn in high heels, but I thought her hair was too dark. I remember thinking that if I could try my new technique on anyone, it would be her.

Later that afternoon Oribe found me in the dispensary. "I know you said you didn't want to work on any models just yet," he said, "but I have someone very special I want you to meet."

Christy had been hovering in the hallway, but now Oribe waved her into the color room where my first reaction was to wonder what the chances were that someone would cancel their appointment that day, that I'd go outside at the precise moment when Christy Turlington was being photographed right in front of the building where I worked, and that an hour later Oribe would introduce me to her. As I look back on my life and career, I realize how many times the universe presented those kinds of opportunities to me, but if I hadn't shown up and done my part, none of those opportunities would have panned out.

Instinctively I knew that I could not do flashy, conspicuous chunks on Christy or she'd freak out. Remembering what Stella Adler said about your choice being your talent, I made the choice to use high-lift tint instead of bleach to create twelve modest, quarter-inch chunks, mostly around her face.

"I love it," she said when she saw the subtle caramel highlights in her light brown hair. "It looks so natural." For Christy, that was important.

What happened next was a tipping point. Clairol asked Oribe and I to do Christy's hair for a magazine ad, and I got a credit: *Color by Brad Johns at Oribe.* Once Christy took the plunge, all the other models wanted me to do their hair too, and because I hadn't scared her away by showing off, Christy trusted me. The next time I did her color, she asked me to go a bit bolder so I used off-the-scalp bleach to give her half-inch chunks. After that, the chunks got bigger and bolder.

Here's what you need to understand about bleach. Marilyn Monroe's double-processed blonde hair required on-the-scalp bleach which, like the name implies, sits on the scalp and can cause irritation. I was using off-the-scalp powder lightener (Clairol Basic White) on Christy, which not only allowed me to achieve more dimension but also

     Brad Johns with Marianne Dougherty

let me regulate the results, lifting each chunk of hair safely from reddish/brown to reddish/orange, orange/yellow to yellow, and, finally, pale yellow to very pale yellow.

Chunking was all about timing, but I never left the results to chance. If I set the timer for ten minutes, I always checked the color after six. Then, once I had the process down, it was as if instinct took over and I didn't rely on the timer anymore.

When I was a little boy, I asked my grandmother how she knew when her pies were ready to come out of the oven. "The longer you do something, the better you understand the process," she told me. "That's where the mystery comes in."

In those early days with Oribe, hair color was still in its infancy. Up until then, women might have colored their hair to cover gray, but they didn't want anyone to know about it. In the 1950s when Clairol introduced Miss Clairol Hair Color Bath, the presumption was that only street walkers or actresses colored their hair. To overcome the stigma, the ad agency Foot, Cone & Belding hired copywriter Shirley Polykoff, a natural blonde who had been dying her hair since she was fifteen to keep it from becoming too dark but had kept that fact a secret for obvious reasons. Her ad copy, which is still a classic, posed the question, "Does she or doesn't she?" before quickly providing the answer: "Only her hairdresser knows for sure."

The ads helped to change perception, and in the 1960s and '70s women had no compunction about dying their hair, though most of them bought boxed hair color at the drugstore and did it themselves. I like to think that what I did twenty years later was elevate hair color to an art form that required a professional.

I have always believed that any woman can be lighter and brighter, and soon editors began calling me the "golden boy." Before long I was seeing forty clients a day: women who might be wearing a watch from Cartier or carrying a Gucci bag, but my hair color? That became the accessory they never took off.

     Brad Johns with Marianne Dougherty

18

had gone to the New School in the 1970s to learn to make jewelry and had an incredible teacher who fabricated the pieces I designed. We used to go to Germany together to buy stones, and she encouraged me to take classes at Parsons School of Design so I could become a silversmith. Dissatisfied with the quality of hair accessories like combs, pins and barrettes that were on the market, I decided to make my own.

Oribe not only built an elaborate display case for my hair jewelry in the salon, but he refused to take a percentage of the profits when the pieces started to sell. I don't think I've ever known anyone as generous as him.

As artists, we were in sync from the very beginning, and we collaborated on projects ranging from photo shoots for fashion magazines like *Vogue* or *Harper's Bazaar* to advertising campaigns for Clairol. Oribe had aligned himself with the best makeup artists and photographers in the business, and we worked almost exclusively with them.

Steven Meisel was achieving critical acclaim for his work in *Vogue* and his photographs of Madonna for her 1992 book *Sex*, but he had started his career as an illustrator for Halston. Suspecting that illustration was on its way out, he accepted an invitation to photograph some models for a booker at Elite Model Management, who admired his illustrations. Keeping his day job working for *Women's*

Wear Daily, he began taking photographs of models on the weekends. One of them was Phoebe Cates, who had begun modeling for magazines like *Seventeen* when she was ten years old and would go on to appear in films like *Fast Times at Ridgemont High* and *Bright Lights, Big City*. Now her portfolio contained Steven's photographs, some of which caught the attention of *Seventeen* who asked if he wanted to work with them. It was one of those fork-in-the-road moments that I have experienced in my own career, and it made all the difference.

Francois Nars, arguably one of the most successful makeup artists in the world, began doing editorial work in 1984 when Polly Mellen, fashion editor at *Vogue*, took him under her wing. During the early '90s he began working with fashion designers like Marc Jacobs, who had left Perry Ellis to start his own line, and Anna Sui, shaving off model Kristen McMenamy's eyebrows for one of her runway shows. It was a daring move, but Oribe and Steven shared his aesthetic, which would come to define fashion for the next decade.

For Oribe, fashion was all about artifice; hair was sculpture for him. He'd ask me to dye bangs in eight different colors, and when he'd choose a shade and plop it onto Christy's head, you could hear the editors in the audience gasping, "Christy's got blonde bangs!"

His collaboration with Gianni Versace is legendary. The two of them had a synergy that was palpable, and throughout the '90s they collaborated on photo shoots, ad campaigns and runway shows. Perhaps Versace's bright colors and prints reminded Oribe of his native Cuba, but he admired the designer so much that he had tattooed sleeves in vibrant colors, an homage to the designer's bold designs, on both arms. As usual Oribe was ahead of the curve, pioneering a look that would be embraced by pop stars like Justin Bieber, John Mayer, Adam Levine and Travis Barker.

It was always exciting when the designers began showing him their ideas for the next season. "New fashion is coming!" he'd announce, and I knew I'd be required to replicate the colors in each collection on wigs that Oribe would pile one on top of the other to create towering works of art.

I had a new boyfriend named Roberto, who was hired as an assistant fresh out of beauty school. The two of us would take Oribe's entire collection of wigs back to my apartment and pin each one to the wall. I'd apply the color, and we'd watch rivulets of bright orange or red or pink drip down the stark white walls. I doubt I'll ever forget the thrill of watching models walk the runway wearing my art during Fashion Week.

Meghan Douglas was one of the top models at the time. She had beautiful blue eyes, almost catlike, but her hair was a muted shade of brown. I decided that she should be a redhead. When she walked the runway in that color in 1995, everyone took notice, including Helene Curtis, which offered her a television and print campaign for Finesse Shampoo and Conditioner that made her a star.

Meanwhile, beauty editors began calling me for interviews. I was naïve enough at first to believe that they were interested in my art, but they were only calling because I did models and celebrities, and that's what their readers were interested in. Gossip columnists like Walter Winchell in the 1930s and '40s and then later Cindy Adams fueled celebrity culture writing about movie stars, but in the '90s someone like me could become a celebrity simply by virtue of which famous clients sat in my chair. After editors began referring to me as a "celebrity colorist," *People* magazine wrote a profile about me.

As my star continued to rise, I got a call from an editor at my hometown newspaper, *The Pittsburgh Press*. She asked a lot of questions about my childhood before we talked about what it was like to work at Oribe's salon where my clients included some of the most beautiful women in the world. The takeaway from my rags-to-riches story with its reference to the "dismal housing project" where I grew up was that hard work and perseverance enabled me to achieve the American Dream, and I guess it had.

I was generating a lot of publicity in those days, but my grandmother didn't read *Vogue* or *Allure*. She tossed the *Enquirer* into her cart when she was shopping for groceries. Imagine how excited she was when she saw my name in the tabloid. That was a big deal to her.

I was so busy at the salon that I needed a break every now and then. On a whim I booked a week at Cal-a-Vie, a wellness retreat near San Diego where I met Ellen Rakieten, who co-created and produced *The Oprah Winfrey Show*. Ellen had an instinct for discovering new products which Oprah endorsed on her show. Those endorsements had the power to influence public opinion and boost sales of everything from Spanx to Uggs. The phenomenon became known as "The Oprah Effect." Now I was about to be discovered.

I met Ellen at the pool one afternoon. She knew who I was because she'd seen my picture is some magazine or another. She and Oprah were on vacation with a few other people, including Oprah's longtime hairdresser, Andre Walker, and her makeup artist, Reggie Wells. I ended up spending a lot of time with them that week, and before we all went home, Ellen invited me to do a makeover segment on Oprah's show with Oribe, Frederic Fekkai and the makeup artist Kevyn Aucoin.

The four of us went to Chicago to do makeovers on Oprah's staff, and it was the most fun I ever had. When Oprah introduced me to her audience for the first time, she told them, "This is Brad Johns, one of the finest colorists in the world."

Hadn't that been my goal since I worked at Clive Summers and defined my mission in no uncertain terms? I always say that the universe is like McDonald's: When it's time to place your order, you won't get apple pie if you don't ask for it.

— 19 —

While I was at Oribe, a lot of models and celebrities sat in my chair, and some of them became good friends. One of them was Kate Moss, a rail-thin British model who became part of a fashion trend called "heroin chic" that enjoyed a brief run in the early 1990s.

Kate had been discovered when she was fourteen. Two years later she was photographed for *The Face,* a British music, fashion and culture magazine. Melanie Ward, who styled the shoot, described the photographs as "dirty realism" or "grunge." So, it's no surprise that Marc Jacobs booked her to walk the runway in 1993 when he presented the "grunge collection" that got him fired from Perry Ellis.

Fashionistas hated the collection, which included printed granny dresses and silk shirts designed to look like flannel. Instead of stilettos, models wore Dr. Martens. The British journalist and fashion critic Suzy Menkes wrote, "Grunge is ghastly," and Oribe agreed with her. When he and Kevyn Aucoin were hired to do hair and makeup for the show, they received very specific instructions: *No hair and no makeup.* Years later looking back on that period, Oribe told a reporter for *The New York Times,* "Grunge was a sad day for all of us." He told me that he prayed every night, "God, let it be over."

The atmosphere at Oribe's salon was like a high-end nightclub where celebrities mingled with regular clients. It was all very egalitarian, and everyone got along. One day when Kate was in my chair, she asked if I'd be willing to go to her boyfriend's apartment and color his hair.

I was so busy that I just didn't pay attention to who one celebrity or another was dating so I had no idea who Kate's boyfriend was, but I knew that Chris would because he read all the scandal mags. "Johnny Depp," he told me with a perceptible eye roll.

When we met, Johnny had begun accepting parts in independent films, and he was in New York to prepare for his role in *Donnie Brasco* as FBI undercover agent Joseph D. Pistone, who infiltrated the Bonnano crime family in New York City during the 1970s. The studio was paying for an apartment in the city while he prepped for the film.

When I arrived at his apartment for the first time, I expected to find an entourage camped out there. The door was unlocked so I let myself in. The place was empty, and after a few minutes Johnny wandered into the living room in tight jeans, barefoot and shirtless.

"Oh, no you don't," I warned him. "You need to put your shirt on. I can't stare at your bare chest all afternoon."

"I like you already," he told me before going into the bedroom to find something to wear.

We became friends after that, and I went back to his apartment to touch up his color every two weeks during filming. I was lifting weights in those days, and Johnny used to tease me. If I was wearing a sleeveless shirt, he'd say, "Look at Brad's guns."

One day I walked in and found the real Donnie Brasco cooking spaghetti in the kitchen like it was nothing out of the ordinary. Sometimes Kate would be there, and the two of them chain-smoked while I worked.

Johnny's natural hair color is light brown, but he needed to look the part so I made his hair a dark chestnut shade. It's a cliché that all Italian men have black hair. I should know since I grew up in an Italian family. I also knew that if I dyed his hair black, it would look like shoe polish under the lights. Fortunately, Johnny trusted me and told the studio that he wanted me to touch up his color instead of having someone on set do it.

While I didn't do his color for the film *Fear and Loathing in Las Vegas* (Johnny played gonzo journalist Hunter S. Thompson), he invited me to the premiere. Johnny and I did a couple of other films together, including *The Brave*, which he directed. He played a Native American named Raphael who agrees to star in a snuff film to provide for his family. The subject matter was really dark, and the film received mostly negative reviews from the critics, which is why Johnny did not release it in theaters in the United States.

When he played Spencer Armacost, an astronaut working for NASA in the 1999 science fiction thriller *The Astronaut's Wife*, he hired me to dye his hair blonde (his idea). I remember him telling me that they had discovered this new actress to play his wife and she was so beautiful. Her name was Charlize Theron.

I had some trepidation about working with Iggy Pop because he had a reputation for being difficult, but Oribe asked me to bleach his hair white-blonde for a project he was doing. Reluctantly, I agreed, but we got along really well. Before he left the salon, he shouted loud enough for anyone within earshot to hear, "You are the smoking-est dude uptown."

Patty Hearst came in for color one day, but her name did not ring a bell when I saw it on the books. Vivian

       Brad Johns with Marianne Dougherty

reminded me that she was the granddaughter of publishing tycoon William Randolph Hearst and had been kidnapped by the radical Symbionese Liberation Army in 1974 when she was nineteen years old. That's when I recalled seeing photographs of her taking part in a bank robbery in San Francisco with other members of the militant group. Her hair was long and dark, and she was carrying an assault rifle.

We never talked about her storied past, but we both agreed that she should be a blonde. For the heir to a family fortune, she was very sweet and told me to do whatever I thought best. When she left the salon that day, her shoulder-length hair was golden blonde with lighter chunks of color around the face. After that, she came back to see me every three weeks, and each time we went blonder and blonder. By the time she played Juror #8 in *Serial Mom*, her hair was as light as it ever would be.

Like Lucille Ball, Carol Burnett was another comedienne born to be a redhead. Red hair suited her. She favored a cherry-red shade I called "Carol Burnett Red," but she allowed me to make the color a bit lighter. Later she confessed that she just wasn't comfortable as a strawberry blonde, and I took her back to "Carol Burnett Red."

When I told her that her show was one of the bright spots in my childhood, she fixed me with a wide smile. "Well, aren't you nice."

Later on, she was gracious enough to mention me in an interview in *People* magazine, and I quote: "Brad has a nice sink-side manner." I loved that my sink-side manner was what impressed her, but it made sense once you knew her. Carol Burnett is a person who cares very deeply about others and recognizes the importance of treating people with respect.

Now that I was on the A-list, I was invited to a party for Madonna's provocative book, *Sex*, at Industria Studios. The guest of honor was dressed like a little girl in pigtails, and every now and then she'd lick a lollypop suggestively.

My grandmother, who had been doing some family tree research, had discovered that we were related to "the virgin." That's how she referred to Madonna.

"You know, the one who sings about being a virgin," she said. "She's a Ciccone like us."

I'd been given access to the VIP area so I approached "the virgin" and told her we were third cousins.

"That's great!" she trilled, though I'm not sure she believed me.

I was invited to another exclusive event that I'll never forget. Ralph Pucci International is a luxury furniture, lighting and mannequin company based in New York City, and one year they held a party at their showroom featuring fifty mannequins that all looked like Christy Turlington, who had posed for master sculptor Michael Evert. Christy gave one of those mannequins, which are worth thousands of dollars today, to Oribe.

Every year *Vogue* hosts an exclusive party to mark the opening of the Costume Institute's exhibition at the Metropolitan Museum of Art. The event is strictly black-tie, but one year I went with one of Oribe's bookers and some people from Chrome Hearts, the luxury brand founded by motorcycle enthusiast Richard Stark. When we all arrived in full leather, not black-tie, a lot of people were displeased with the affront, but at least we were wearing black. I met Louis Licari, one of the world's leading colorists, at that party. I admired him because he had trained as a painter at Syracuse University and had an artist's eye for color.

     Brad Johns with Marianne Dougherty

Charla Krupp, the fashion and beauty commentator, became a good friend, and when her book *How Not to Look Old* was published, I went to her book party, which attracted icons like Christy Brinkley, Debbie Harry and Lulu, who sang the theme song for the film *To Sir, With Love*. I adored Lulu, who was married to the British hairdresser John Frieda, and when he was looking for someone to represent his new hair color line, I took a meeting just so I could ask him about his wife. *Is her hair really red? What's she like? Are you happily married? Do you have any children?* I was like a teenage fan peppering him with questions.

After a few years at Oribe, I started making one of the first of any number of trips to Los Angeles, rearranging my schedule so I could spend a couple of weeks there. On one of those visits, I went to see Giuseppe Franco at his salon in Beverly Hills. The two of us had worked together at Jean Louis David in New York in the 1970s and were hired to work on the teen comedy-drama *Little Darlings* starring Kristy McNichol and Tatum O'Neal. I permed Kristy's hair while Giuseppe styled both actresses.

When we arrived in Atlanta, Tatum noticed that I had a blue streak in my hair and called out, "Oh, look, we have a punk rock hairdresser."

Giuseppe's best friend was Mickey Rourke, who helped finance his salon. Mickey was dating the actress Carrie Otis then, and the four of us went out almost every night while I was in Los Angeles. We often had dinner at Chaya Brasserie, a popular French-Asian fusion restaurant in West Hollywood where Japanese parasols spun from the ceiling. Mickey always picked up the tab even if I offered to pay.

I never charged celebrities in those days, but when I foiled very medium-blonde highlights into Mickey's hair, he pressed five crisp one hundred dollar bills into my hand. Johnny Depp was generous like that as well.

Years later when I had my own salon, Tatum showed up. She was married to John McEnroe at the time, and they were living in a five-building estate in Cove Neck, New York. While we reminisced about the first time we met, I lightened up her whole head to a dark golden blonde and put big gold pieces all over. She loved what I did and became a regular client for a few years.

Matthew Modine and Kristen Johnston (3rd *Rock from the Sun*) are still friends today. I met Matthew when I was Global Color Director at Avon Salon and Spa, probably in 2001 or so. He was having his hair cut there, and his stylist suggested that he see me for color. Both of us were obsessed with movies. When he was growing up in Loma Linda, California, his father managed the local drive-in, and he worked there in the summer. We tend to like the same movies, and we have high standards. When we saw a film that critics loved but we abhorred, we called it a classic case of the emperor's new clothes. Why had none of them seen that the film was, clearly, terrible?

My favorite of all Matthew's films is *Birdy*. I think he should have won an Oscar for that performance, but he takes those kinds of things in stride. "It's just show business," he tells me when he loses a role to someone else or isn't nominated for some award or another.

Matthew married Caridad Rivera, a Puerto Rican makeup artist and wardrobe stylist, in 1980, and they are still madly in love after all these years. Matthew adores her, and it doesn't take much to make him jealous. A man turning to stare as Cari walks down the street will do it, but she is always quick to reassure him, "You know I'm all yours."

		Brad Johns with Marianne Dougherty

Kristen Johnston is one of the funniest, loveliest people I've ever met. She had been blonde as a child so I made her hair really, really blonde. In 2012, I went to a book signing for her memoir, *Guts*, which chronicles her addiction and ultimate sobriety. It's hilarious, like she is, but also heartbreaking. I was flattered when she included me in the Acknowledgments. Kristen taught me that sobriety doesn't have to be boring; you can be sober and still be funny and fabulous.

In 2003 when Vanessa Redgrave was on Broadway in *Long Day's Journey Into Night*, I colored her hair, which had to be grey for the role. We talked a lot about her beautiful daughter Natasha Richardson, who had not only been my client but also a close friend. When we first started seeing each other socially, it was usually to go to the theater together.

One day Natasha came into the salon to tell me that she'd been offered the role of Sally Bowles in a revival of *Cabaret,* which was set to open on Broadway on in March, 1998. All my instincts told me that she needed to be uber-blonde to play the iconic chanteuse, and she agreed.

"You're going to win a Tony," I told her.

"Absolutely not," she insisted, but when I saw her come onstage in that white-blonde hair and sing "Maybe This Time," I knew she'd win. Natasha was very self-deprecating. I don't think she was ever satisfied with a performance, and she invited me backstage on opening night because she knew I'd be honest with her.

Placing one hand over her heart, she said, "So, how was I?" I couldn't believe she had to ask.

When she was nominated for a Tony, just as I knew she would be, I made her hair even lighter for the ceremony. "I am completely stunned," she said as she accepted her award, but I wasn't.

One year I was invited to one of her birthday parties at a private club in Manhattan. Her husband, actor Liam Neeson was there, of course, and so was her mother and her aunt, Lynn Redgrave. I caught a glimpse of Uma Thurman and Sarah Jessica Parker, who came with Tracy Pollan and Michael J. Fox. Kristen Johnston and Matthew Modine were there, too.

I had brought a date who was a lot younger than me, and I gave him instructions not to point or stare. Dumbstruck, he whispered, "These are all famous people."

I would have killed to do Gwyneth Paltrow's hair, which I envisioned as a surfer-blonde shade, and after a few drinks I worked up the courage to approach her. If memory serves, I dropped one of my business cards into the neckline of her low-cut dress, a move that was, in retrospect, decidedly *declasse*.

Later Natasha took me aside. "Brad, you didn't have to give her your card. She knows who you are."

I was shocked. *Gwyneth Paltrow knows who I am?*

"We're here to celebrate my birthday," Natasha reminded me, "and you've been invited because you're my friend just as much as anyone else in this room."

It was a powerful lesson for someone like me who had been hustling his whole life; that's how I rose to the top of my profession. Clive Summers taught me about self-promotion when I worked for him. It was like a game we played. I'd take a client whose color I had just done over to his station to show her off.

"Lovely, just lovely, Brad," he'd say in his tony British accent. Meanwhile, three of his clients waiting to have their hair cut would turn around to take a look, and I'd have three new color clients by the end of the day. I got very busy that way, and I have Clive to thank for that. He built my career.

Natasha was like having a sophisticated, younger sister to show you the ropes. She took me under her wing and taught me about how to navigate the world of the rich and famous. Having grown up in London, she learned how to behave in what people used to call "polite society," and her mother had taught her the importance of good manners. One time we went to the theater together and she took me backstage. One of the actors was a friend of hers, and even though we both agreed that the performance was dreadful, she never said an unkind word.

"By then it was a *fait accompli*," she explained, "so what's the point?"

I did Natasha's hair color right before she left for her ill-fated ski trip to Quebec in March, 2009. She had taken a lesson and fell at the base of the beginners' trail, striking her head. The instructor was worried enough to call for an ambulance, but she said she'd be fine. By three o'clock when she seemed disoriented and complained of a headache, she was taken to a nearby hospital, which was ill-equipped to treat her. Three hours later she was transferred to a Montreal trauma center. By the time Liam arrived, doctors could find no sign of brain activity.

In an interview with Anderson Cooper for CNN, he admitted that he and Natasha had made a pact that if one of them was incapacitated, the other would "pull the plug." Honoring his wife's wish not to be kept alive by artificial means, he had her transported to Lenox Hill Hospital in New York City where friends and family were at her bedside when she was removed from life support. She was forty-five years old.

I did not go to her funeral, but the day after she died, I was meditating in my apartment on Perry Street in the West Village when I sensed a presence in the room. I opened my eyes and there she was: a translucent figure sitting on the arm of the sofa, one leg crossed over the other, her cheek resting in the palm of her hand, a pose I'd seen her strike many times before.

"Natasha, what are you doing here?" I asked her.

"We had a lot of fun together, didn't we?" she said. "Thank you for making me look so beautiful."

Then she was gone, as ephemeral as a snowfall in spring.

20

O wning my own salon had never been the goal, but some-times when opportunity knocks, it's best to answer the door. In 1995 a group of investors approached me about opening a three-story salon in the Takashimaya Building that would be unlike anything else in the city. Located on Fifth Avenue between the prestigious St. Regis-Sheraton Hotel and the former Aeolian Building, the Takashimaya Building is considered a masterpiece of craftsmanship, and my name would appear in brass letters on the granite façade, a first for any hairdresser.

At first, I was afraid to tell Oribe about the offer because I was bringing in a lot of money. I thought he'd be angry if I left, but he encouraged me to go out on my own and see what the future held in store. So, I accepted the offer and work began on the project, which cost nearly seven million dollars.

Almost every item in the salon was fabricated from rubber, aluminum or Plexiglas. The color scheme was black, white and silver. I had stopped using capital letters after I saw Laura Nyro sign her name in lowercase, and that's how my name appeared on everything, including handmade jewelry in silver and gold embellished with Swarovski crystals. Shampoo and conditioner with my sister's favorite scent, lily of the valley, were packaged in translucent white bottles. If you held them up to the light, you could see exactly how much product was left. I hired an esthetician to do facials, and my name was on every skincare product we carried. I also designed a line of makeup and packaged shades to flatter blondes, brunettes or redheads in black lacquer cases embossed with my name in gold.

To celebrate, the investors threw a party at the salon in February, 1996. Benjamin Liu, who was Andy Warhol's personal and studio assistant, planned the party, and if your name was not on the guest list, you didn't get in. A stickler for details, he also created a mixtape of my favorite songs, which played in a loop all evening.

I commissioned a handmade leather jumpsuit (one half was white, the other half black) from a designer who made clothing for all the rock stars, and I wore one black shoe and one white shoe with pointy toes and high heels from Ian's.

A lot of models were in Paris for fashion week, but Meghan Douglas and Tricia Helfer came. So did the fashion and beauty press. Most of my family was there that night: my mother and father, of course, but also Craig and Shari, my aunt Alice and my cousin Lynn. My friend Jim (we went to grade school together) took the train up from Baltimore where he was living at the time. Sparky, my babysitter and muse, showed up in the same stark-white hair she had when we lived at OVA, but now she was carrying a Louis Vuitton bag. Like me, she had put her impoverished childhood behind her.

My new boyfriend, a gorgeous Puerto Rican bodybuilder I'd met at the gym, was stunning in white pants and a white T-shirt, a heavy silver chain around his neck.

I remember being in a lot of pain that night due to complications from hernia surgery. I don't think anyone knew what I was going through. The place was mobbed,

     Brad Johns with Marianne Dougherty

and I was giving one interview after another. It was chaotic. My mother had indulged in one too many Cosmopolitans (she thought they were some kind of fruit punch), and by the time I got to the party she was three sheets to the wind.

I don't think I've ever seen anyone as beautiful without makeup as Carolyn Bessette Kennedy except for Christy Turlington. Carolyn had remained a loyal client and friend, and it meant a lot to me that she was willing to brave the phalanx of photographers outside just to be there on my big night. I had told so many stories about my mother over the years that Carolyn was eager to meet her. Someone found two chairs for them, and a couple of security guards kept watch so they wouldn't be disturbed. The two of them spent the rest of the evening together, but we didn't have to worry about anyone taking photos surreptitiously on their phones since that technology was a few years away.

Carolyn had married John F. Kennedy, Jr. five months earlier in a private ceremony on a secluded island seven miles off the coast of Georgia. Construction was still in progress on my own salon so I was doing hair at Clive Summers again. Carolyn came in for color the day before her wedding. I knew something was up because her energy was frenetic. She also wanted me to make her hair really dark. We had spent a long time getting her hair to the iconic blonde stage that had become her trademark, and I talked her out of such a drastic change.

"Okay, just do what you want," she said, so we went whiter and lighter.

When I saw a copy of *People* magazine a few days later, I understood why she had been so skittish that day in the salon. On the cover in red type were the words "WELL DONE."

John, reaching for her hand, wears a Gordon Henderson suit, while Carolyn is in a floor-length gown of pearl-white crepe, a hand-rolled tulle silk veil and long white gloves designed by her friend, Narcisco Rodriguez, who she met while at Calvin Klein. She's clutching a simple bouquet of lily of the valley, and her beautiful blonde hair is pulled back in a low chignon. Caught in profile, the way she looks at her new husband says it all. She is deeply in love, and I was happy for her.

I called her a few days later. "How do you think your hair would have looked on the cover of *People* if I'd done what you wanted me to?"

"Thank God I listened to you," she said with a sigh of relief.

Narciso admitted that once that photo appeared in every major newspaper in the world, his life changed irrevocably. On the PBS show *Finding Your Roots*, he told Henry Louis Gates, "I went from being a kinda private person to being a very public person overnight."

The same thing happened to Carolyn. Her new husband was as close to American royalty as you can get, and they couldn't go anywhere without being swamped by paparazzi. We enjoyed each other's company and liked to meet for lunch every now and then, but it was difficult to avoid the photographers who camped out on the street in front of the apartment in Tribeca she shared with John. So, we started meeting at restaurants in the neighborhood where she felt certain our presence would go unnoticed. Occasionally we'd have a waiter who appeared to be eavesdropping on our conversation, and sure enough, the next day there would be an item in *Page Six*, the gossip column in the *New York Post*.

One of the low points of my career came when I received a cease-and-desist letter from John's lawyers. As soon as the press found out I was doing Carolyn's hair, reporters began calling me for interviews. Since we had been friends long before Carolyn married John, she gave me permission to use her name if it would help my career, but apparently her husband felt differently. I can understand that he valued his privacy since he had grown up in the glare of the spotlight, but it was painful for me because I loved Carolyn and was sorry to see our friendship end so abruptly. You have to remember that there was no media training in those days, no one to teach me what was appropriate to say to the press and what wasn't. Maybe I talked about her too much, but I just wanted people to know the Carolyn I knew.

I got a lot of negative press after that, and things got so bad that I contemplated leaving New York and moving back to Pittsburgh. Then I remembered a line from a song by Todd Rundgren: *You can say what you will about me, talk is cheap and I don't mind.* So, I stayed in New York, the press moved on to someone else and slowly things improved.

I was at work on July 16, 1999, when Vivian called to tell me that John's plane was missing. Both Carolyn and her sister Lauren were onboard. I can't explain how I knew, but I felt certain that she was gone. That evening while I was mediating, I received a visitation from Carolyn. That's the only way to describe what happened. Thousands of people have reported experiencing after-death communications in which they felt the presence of a loved who has recently died, usually within the first twenty-four hours. Some people hear voices or detect the scent of a familiar fragrance. For me, it was the sensation that someone was touching the top of my head: one, two, three taps. Carolyn knew that three is my sacred number. The whole experience was profoundly moving and over as quickly as it had begun, but I felt as if my friend had come to say goodbye, and it brought me to tears.

Human intelligence is limited, and there are simply things we don't understand. I am reminded of Hamlet who sees his father's ghost four times, a phenomenon for which there is no logical explanation. His trusted friend Horatio is not inclined to believe in ghosts, but Hamlet addresses the issue in Act 1 Scene 5 when he delivers what may be one the most memorable lines in Shakespeare's play: *There are more things in Heaven and Earth, Horatio, than are dreamt of in your philosophy.*

     Brad Johns with Marianne Dougherty

21

efore we could promote ourselves on social media like Instagram and TikTok, hairdressers had to assemble a portfolio of work good enough to impress beauty editors who would get the word out for us. It didn't hurt if you had a roster of celebrity clients either. I'd been working with celebrities since my days at Cinandre and Clive Summers, but now my work was appearing in magazines like *Vogue* and *Allure*.

By the time I opened my own salon, I was able to cash in on all that publicity. *Vogue* wanted an exclusive, and they broke the news in a four-page story called *Yellow Fever*. In the accompanying photo, I'm dressed in silver lame while a horde of screaming blonde models chase me down the street like I'm one of the Rolling Stones. Having *Vogue* do a profile of me was a milestone, but I knew I'd arrived when I got a call from *People* magazine.

The photographer snapped photos of me in a styling chair, my long blonde hair as light as it had ever been. I had this notion that as you became richer and more famous, your hair had to become blonder. Think Marilyn and Madonna. Blonde hair reads expensive. It's hard to maintain, and it requires the kind of upkeep that doesn't come cheap.

I was doing so well that I thought the ride would never end, but five years later it did. I might have been on one of the classic wooden roller coasters at Kennywood Park in my hometown that jerks to a stop after a breathtaking run filled with hairpin curves and a seventy-foot double-dip drop. Later I learned that the salon was being mismanaged.

After the investors decided to get out of the beauty business, I had to plan my next move. To have a career like I did that spanned decades at the top salons in New York City, you've got to be agile enough to move on quickly and always to something even better.

Avon was rebranding and had opened a four-floor complex in Trump Tower that not only housed a retail store on the first floor but also a full-service salon. So, I placed a call to the general manager, who was more than happy to have my team at Avon where we could burnish the company's image. Initially, I had six chairs and the promise of my own studio, a product line and a retail outlet for my jewelry. It took a couple of years, but Avon made good on all of those promises.

One of the perks of working for a multinational company like Avon was that it had its own laboratories for developing a range of personal care products, and they wanted to create a line of shampoo and conditioner for me. We called it Brad Johns Colorsave. The gold shampoo, which was infused with nourishing sea algae and rosemary extract, added sunny, buttery tones to natural and color-treated shades of blonde hair.

To announce our partnership, Avon hosted a lavish party at Trump Tower. I had insisted on hiring the D.J. Anita Sarko, a fixture at the Mudd Club, which was the antithesis of Studio 54. The idea was to bring a downtown vibe uptown to this corporate environment. When word got out that Natasha Richardson, Matthew Modine and

Kristen Johnston would be there, a lot of press showed up. That's how it works.

While I had been filled with anxiety when my salon closed, working for Avon opened up a whole new world of opportunities. Now I wasn't just getting publicity in fashion and beauty magazines, I was also being featured in *Glamour* and *More* as well as general interest magazines like *Ladies' Home Journal* that reached a wider audience. I loved the fact that I was offering advice to women like my mother or grandmother, who could benefit from the knowledge I'd accumulated during my career.

More magazine asked me to do makeovers on four of their readers for the October 2001 issue. Lois Joy Johnson, who became a good friend, wrote the story called *The Golden Touch*. The feature included a full page of advice from me. *Color and cut are a marriage. Stay away from clarifying shampoos. One solid blonde color without highlights can look dated.* Readers could also enter a contest to win a hair color session with me, and I offered a discount to anyone who booked an appointment and brought their copy of the magazine into the salon with them.

I don't think I was prepared for how many women would do just that, but many of them became longtime clients. What no one knew at the time was that for years I had been offering discounts to people I admired, like nurses, teachers and anyone who worked with special-needs children. I didn't do any of those things because I expected something in return, but the good I did has come back to me tenfold, and I am grateful for everything.

In retrospect, the sheer amount of publicity I was generating in those days seems staggering to me. The editors at *Allure* had been including me on their list of top colorists in the country for a while. Now they were calling me for tips and advice on a regular basis.

A story by Lindsey Von Gelder called *The Coloring Book* was featured in the January 2001 issue. "Tint master Brad Johns mixes up a batch of his best hair color tips," she wrote. Next to a picture of me was this description: *He's been referred to as the "high priest of hair" during his 25 years as a colorist. Now, as artistic director of New York's Avon Centre, Brad Johns lightens and brightens stars like Uma Thurman and Natasha Richardson. We caught up with him between clients and asked him to share his top tinting tips.*

Some of those tips included "Frosting is for cakes, not hair," and "If you want to be a blond, take it to a pro." That's still good advice today if you ask me. I was also adamant that hair be the color of spices (cinnamon or nutmeg) or candy (caramel or butterscotch) and not vegetables (eggplant or cranberries) or wine (burgundy or merlot). I think the editors got a kick out of my proclamations in those days.

I was just as forthcoming with my clients. When I told one of them that she had Nancy Reagan hair, she understood that I was not paying her a compliment and trusted me to fix the problem. Another *faux pas*: highlights that looked like overcooked capellini. And more than once I had to remind a client that what we were doing was hair color, not magic. They must have respected me as an artist and trusted me to tell them the truth because they were loyal to a fault, following me from one salon to another.

While I was at Avon, Clairol approached me about becoming Global Color Director, a position that would include television appearances and print ads. It was easy to recommend their products because I had been using Clairol since beauty school.

     Brad Johns with Marianne Dougherty

I may have grown up in poverty, but I had learned how to accumulate wealth by buying property. I held onto that beach house in Long Beach, New York, that I bought with my Clairol money for five years before deciding to put it on the market. Frankly, I was tired of going to the same place every weekend.

I turned down a couple of offers before I heard God's voice telling me to take the loss and let it go. God had never failed me before so I did what I was told. The house sold in 2011. A year later Hurricane Sandy washed it away.

22

When I was in high school, my friend Jeff took me to the Carnegie Museum of Art in Pittsburgh where he introduced me to the Old Masters and the Impressionists. Remember the story of how Annie Sullivan taught Helen Keller to communicate by pouring water over her hand while she signed the word "water" on her palm? Jeff was my Annie Sullivan. After that visit to the Carnegie Museum, I was no longer blind to the world of art.

Ever since that day, the visual arts—drawing, painting, photography, printmaking, theater—have played an important role in my life. My education continued in New York City, home to the Metropolitan Museum of Art, the Whitney Museum of American Art and the Museum of Modern Art (MoMA). For years I took the train to Beacon, a small town in upstate New York, to visit the Dia Art Foundation (DIA). Founded in 1974 by the German art dealer Heiner Friedrich and his wife, Philippa de Menil, the museum commissioned works by contemporary artists, notably minimalists and conceptual artists, which I love.

I saw a retrospective of the work of Franz Kline at DIA. Born in Wilkes-Barre, a coal mining town in Northeast Pennsylvania, he worked as a designer at a department store in New York City and later became part of the abstract expressionist movement. What I loved about his work, aside from the monochromatic palette, were paintings influenced

        Brad Johns with Marianne Dougherty

by his childhood in the industrial Lehigh Valley that looked like sad, abstract bridges to me. Kline lost his father to suicide when he was seven years old, and after her remarriage, his mother sent him to a college in Philadelphia for fatherless boys. In photographs, you can see the sadness on his face.

For years I have been a big fan of the minimalist Ellsworth Kelly, the American painter, sculptor and printmaker whose style called "hard-edge painting" features geometric shapes with sudden and unexpected transitions between color areas. When he lived in Paris, Kelly discovered Monet's later work and, in 1950, painted *Seine*, which was comprised of black and white rectangles. *The Meschers*, 1951, is a series of green and blue shapes arranged at random. I have one of his prints in my apartment in West Hollywood: a white triangle partially obscuring a black rectangle.

My friendship with Cindy Sherman, one of the most important photographers and artists working today, opened a lot of doors into the art world for me. I met Cindy at MoMA in 1997 at an exhibit of her sixty-nine untitled black-and-white stills, which was sponsored by Madonna. My friend and client Liz Rosenberg invited me to be her plus-one. Liz was not only president of public relations for Warner Bros. Records but also Madonna's publicist.

I knew I'd have to wear something special that night so I commissioned a pair of white leather pants that zipped up the side and a sleeveless white leather vest. To complete my costume, I bought a pair of pointy white leather boots with six-inch heels at Trash and Vaudeville, a boutique on St. Mark's Place that sold clothing to rock stars.

Liz knew that my goal that night was to meet Cindy, and when she saw her standing on the steps surrounded by her adoring public, she gave me a little push. "Go."

Cutting a swath through the crowd like Moses parting the Red Sea, I went right up to Cindy and introduced myself. "I have to do your color," I told her.

"Great," she said without hesitation, and we exchanged numbers.

From that day on, we have been as close as brother and sister. I think we bonded as artists because both of us understood that by immersing ourselves in the creative process we were able to leave all our sadness behind. I wanted to find a studio where I could paint, and Cindy told me about a loft for rent on 26th Street where I began experimenting with vertical art.

For one of my pieces, I bought liquid plastic and mixed it with an elixir, which I dripped onto a piece of Plexiglas so it looked like tears. Then I slipped two extra panels behind the first one so it had a three-dimensional effect. I called that piece *Storms That We Cannot Weather.*

A plastic material made from polymers of methyl methacrylate, Plexiglas was the perfect surface for the kind of painting I wanted to do, but I didn't know anyone else who was working with it. Since I had no one to ask for advice, it took a while to figure out what kind of mask to wear.

Years ago, I had a one-man show at a gallery in New York City of my portraits in acrylic on Plexiglas of Vivian, my mother and father and three of my boyfriends. Then Avon sponsored a show at Trump Tower. We sold all six paintings in a collection I called *Curtains* with proceeds going to benefit cancer research in honor of my mother, who was battling the disease.

The notion that our lives are determined by fate has always intrigued me even though there's no way to prove the theory. What I do know is that because Otto Rohm invented Plexiglas in 1933 and Lawrence Gelb introduced Clairol to the public in 1949, I was able to create art using chemicals that didn't exist until the 20th century.

Cindy taught me to be open-minded about art, especially if I was resistant to something new. That's how I discovered Bill Viola, a contemporary video artist whose work focuses of human experiences like birth, death and the unfolding of consciousness. I hated video, had no time for it, but I agreed to see one of his exhibits. Now I'm a big fan. A graduate of the College of Visual and Performing Arts at Syracuse University, Viola has been creating videotapes, architectural video installations and sound environments for forty years, drawing on Eastern and Western art as well as Zen Buddhism, Islamic Sufism and Christian mysticism, all of which speak to me on a profoundly basic level, yet I would have missed out on that experience had I not taken Cindy's advice and kept an open mind about art I did not understand at first.

Cindy has invited me to a lot of events or private parties over the years where I've met some of the artists whose work I admire most: the director John Waters; the conceptual photographer and artist Sara Charlesworth; visual artist Marilyn Minter, whose works blur the line between commercial and fine art; Lisa Yuskavage, who is known for her bold, eccentric figure paintings; the conceptual artist and collagist Barbara Kruger; Eric Fischl, who gained renown for his colorful paintings of American suburban culture from the 1970s to the 1980s, and his wife, the artist April Gornik; Elizabeth Peyton, known for her intimate portraits of celebrities, friends and historical figures; and the international art critic and journalist Linda Yablonsky. I admired her because she didn't sugarcoat anything. If she didn't like a work of art or the artist, she said so.

I have always thought of what I do as a colorist as being an art form, though I'd place it low on the totem pole after painting, photography and sculpture. Still, these artists I met at dinner parties at Cindy's house in Manhattan respected me enough to come to the salon and let me express my creativity on a living canvas, their hair. I think it finally dawned on me that I'd made it in New York when Cindy took me as her plus-one to black-tie functions where I'd be sitting at a table with celebrities like Elton John or the photographer Nan Goldin, whose candid photographs have documented everything from the HIV crisis to the Opiod epidemic.

Parties at Cindy's house were an eclectic mix of people from artists to art dealers to gallery owners. Klaus Biesenback, the Director of MoMA, came to one of those parties. I was speechless when he introduced me to the Paris-based art historian Diana Picasso, Pablo Picasso's granddaughter. Here I was, a poor kid from the projects, rubbing elbows with some of the greatest artists on the planet.

At a Christmas party at Cindy's house one year, I approached Marilyn Minter. I'd gone to see a retrospective of her work at the Brooklyn Museum and told her how much I admired her.

"Oh, you're Cindy's colorist," she said before leaning in to ask me if I thought she should go blonde. As much as I would have loved doing a makeover on Marilyn Minter, I felt that her dark brown hair fit her personality as an artist and told her so. I think she respected me for being honest.

Cindy loved prowling the flea markets in the Hamptons for props she could use in her art, and we often went together if I was staying at her place for the weekend. Something as mundane as a ski hat with a ball on top might catch her eye, and I'd ask what she planned to do with it.

"I don't know. I just think I need it," she'd tell me, and sure enough, that ski hat would show up in one of her photographs. On one of our excursions, I found a vintage board game based on *The Patty Duke Show*. Patty Duke played identical cousins, Patty and Cathy.

She sighed dramatically. "What do you plan to do with that?"

"We're playing it when we get back to your house," I told her. "You're Cathy and I'm Patty." She threw me a look, but I knew she'd humor me.

Over the years I've applied a lot of what I've learned about art to my work as a colorist. Artists use perspective to create the illusion of depth on a flat surface. By adding highlights to a base color, I was able to do the same thing. Just as Leonardo da Vinci, Rembrandt, Vermeer and Caravaggio famously used light and shadow to great effect in their paintings, my fascination with the way light changes from season to season informed all of my decisions when it came to hair color. My clients knew the rules: the warmer the season, the paler the hair; the colder the season, the warmer the hair. The rules differed slightly for California girls, who could be blonde in January, just not white-blonde. I'd warm up their color to the shade of wheat since the light in January is blue on the West Coast, not yellow like it is in the spring and summer.

Today I am what you might call a serious art collector, and when I moved to Los Angeles, I spent a good deal of time with a decorator before deciding where to hang the art I own. Placing each piece in exactly the right place was like telling a story, the story of my life through the artists who had a big impact on me. From what I've observed, people buy art for different reasons. For a lot of wealthy people, it's an investment. For others it's because the color scheme matches their living room drapes. Cindy taught me that art must move you, period.

So, when you enter my apartment, the first thing you'll see is three prints of Joni Mitchell. One is a black-and-white photograph by David Gahr. She's waving at the camera and looks happy. Another one was the cover of *For the Roses*, which was shot by Joel Bernstein. The third is a portrait by Henry Diltz circa 1970. She's leaning out the window of the house she shared with Graham Nash in Laurel Canyon. Joni Mitchell has always represented California to me, and when I see those prints as I walk in the door, I feel like she is welcoming me home: *I'm your biggest fan, California I'm coming home.*

If at all possible, I do things in threes. Three is a powerful number for me. Not only does it represent the Holy Trinity, but Craig, Shari and I are a threesome. So were my grandmother, my mother and my aunt Alice. The provocative filmmaker John Waters created a series of photographs of Liz Taylor's eyes that he called *Cockeyed*. I have three of them framed as a triptych.

My latest acquisition is a large portrait of Mary called *The Mother of Sorrows* by a young artist named Conner Meager, who I met at Allgorithim, an art gallery on Melrose Avenue in West Hollywood. Brows furrowed, eyes going soft, Mary's expression is one of profound heartache and sadness. What had Cindy told me? Buy art that moves you? This piece of art moved me deeply so I bought it. Incidentally, Mother of Sorrows is the name of the Catholic Church where my spiritual journey began when I was a young boy and my aunt Alice took me to mass with her.

Let's move on to the kitchen where you'll see Andy Warhol contemporary Neke Carson's neon "I Love You." In

     Brad Johns with Marianne Dougherty

his book, *Trickster Makes This World*, Lewis Hyde described Carson as a "boundary-crosser." If nothing else, he defied convention. Warhol filmed the artist bending over a canvas, a paintbrush in his ass. The finished product, a portrait of Warhol, became part of what Carson called his "Rectal Realism" period.

Now, moving into the hallway, you'll have to look closely to read the script on a piece by the English artist Tracy Emin, who is known for her autobiographical confessional artwork. On Mondrian hotel stationery are the words: *I think of you sometimes, and sometimes I dream of you in my sleep.* They're significant because I stayed at the Mondrian Los Angeles with someone I cared for while my apartment was being finished.

A few steps further down the hall is another piece by John Waters called *Boys Beware*, which features clips from an anti-homosexual film from the 1960s. That one is fairly self-explanatory for a gay man like myself who came of age when homosexuality was still prosecuted as a crime. Finally, we come to the painting by Ellsworth Kelly I mentioned earlier.

Once you enter my bedroom, you're in a world of black and white, my favorite color (or non-color) combination. One wall is painted black, and that's where I've placed three more pieces by John Waters: photographs he took of stills from the 1959 film, *Blue Denim*, which starred Brandon de Wilde and Carol Lynley as teenagers whose lives are upended when she becomes pregnant. Its subject matter, which dealt with themes like unexpected pregnancy and abortion, was scandalous for its time. It's a classic story that played out in real life for me and my high school girlfriend.

Closer to my bed are three stainless steel bullet-hole paintings (there's the number three again) by Margaret

Evangeline, a New York-based painter and performance artist who grew up in Louisiana. When I met her in New York some years ago, she explained that the art was not the bullet-riddled pieces themselves but the sound the bullets made as they disturbed the silence in the woods where she fired the gun. "You can't capture that sound in a painting," she explained.

Mounted above my bed is a negative image of the cover of Bowie's *Alladin Sane* by Henry Diltz, but the first thing I see when I wake up is an enormous photograph of Laura Nyro by David Gahr. On the same wall is another piece by Conner Meager called *The Man of Man*: a black-and-white pixelated portrait of Christ's face, his bleeding heart exposed. Working on canvas with eggshell paint/primer, spray paint and alcohol paint, he set out to render a "sense of safety, a restoration of faith." Raised Catholic like me, Conner Meager became disillusioned with the church, yet he never let go of his belief in God. He describes *The Man of Man* as "the real artist painting our canvas of the world, rendering meaning where necessary." Again, art that moved me.

In the guest bedroom, which I call the Cindy Sherman room, are gifts she gave me over the years, including a swimming pool float with her FaceTuned portrait on it (I taught her how to use the app) and books of hers she signed for me. Drake, the Canadian rapper and songwriter, is an important artist for me, and I have several pieces of clothing from his line on a hall tree. On another hall tree are fifteen motorcycle jackets that range in color from silver to black, pink to light blue, and navy blue to medium blue. Four of them are white; two are leather and two are plastic. I wear all of them.

When I was growing up in OVA, I had a poster from the film *Endless Summer* on my wall. Those surfers carrying

     Brad Johns with Marianne Dougherty

their boards into a ball of yellow sun represented California to me, a place I hoped to live one day. Now that I do live in California, I have one of the last three of the original silk-screened posters in the guest bathroom. It's signed by John van Hamersveld, who created the Day-Glo movie promo for his friend Bruce Brown's 1964 documentary.

You have to close the bathroom door to catch a glimpse of one of Brigid Berlin's pink "tit prints." She was a rich girl who grew up in Connecticut and became part of Andy Warhol's Factory. I met her when she was having her hair cut by one of the hairdressers I worked with at Clive Summers. When I told her I had one of those prints, she asked me, "Why would you buy one of those?" as if I'd wasted my money, but I loved the idea of someone being brash enough to dip her tits in paint for all the world to see. If that isn't art, I don't know what is.

Finally, there's a self-portrait of actress Kim Novak, one of Hitchcock's iconic blondes, which I bought from the actress herself.

If my friend Jeff was still alive, I'd thank him for changing my life, for being my Annie Sullivan. Since I can't tell him myself, I choose to believe that he knows. That he's always known how much he meant to me.

23

'd been at Avon for six years, which is a pretty good run, when the company decided to shutter the salon. Again, another door was closing. What I didn't know was that another door was about to open, and this one was red.

Elizabeth Arden's signature "Red Door" salon had been the inspiration for the fictional salon in *The Women*, a 1939 film starring Joan Crawford and Norma Shearer. Like me, Elizabeth Arden (her real name was Florence Nightingale Graham) grew up in poverty before finding her calling: to make women feel beautiful. When she and Elizabeth Hubbard opened a salon on Fifth Avenue in 1909, they painted the door bright red so it would stand out among the other shops in the neighborhood. The story goes that after they dissolved their partnership, Elizabeth scraped Hubbard's last name off the sign and added the word "Arden" from Alfred Lord Tennyson's poem, *Enoch Arden*.

After assuming a new identity as Elizabeth Arden, Florence Nightingale Graham made history by introducing the concept of the "makeover" and creating an empire. By the time she died in 1966 at the age of eighty-seven, she was a millionaire many times over, and her salon was synonymous with luxury and refinement.

Oribe knew Elizabeth Arden's history. That's why he opened his first salon behind those legendary red doors. It's why my first call after Avon closed was to the general manager at Elizabeth Arden, who offered to build me a studio with a wall of windows overlooking Fifth Avenue. The décor was black and white, and I had a case for my jewelry. I'd also started making things that people could display in their homes, like clay hearts on silver chains inscribed with the words "faith, hope and charity." People began buying them as talismans.

Coming to work every morning, I was struck by the thought that I'd come full circle. Miss Arden's portrait on the wall just outside of my office was reassuring, and I sensed that she was watching over me. There was a plaque on another wall that described me as "the golden boy, the founding father of color chunks, the color czar."

To announce my arrival, the company compiled a video of all the press I'd gotten over the years. It ran in a loop in the window of the retail store on the first floor so anyone passing by would see it. It was all very intoxicating, and I had a good six or seven years there, but in 2011when Elizabeth Arden closed the flagship salon, it was back to square one.

Because of my reputation, I was able to land on my feet, yet I began to realize that each transition had taken an emotional toll, triggering painful memories of cowering under the kitchen table with my brother while the rent collector pounded on the front door. Our fear then was that we'd be evicted. Homeless. Now those feelings resurfaced every time I had to find a new place to work.

If I had still been doing drugs, I might have gotten high to deal with the anxiety, but I had been clean for a while. Instead, I went inward, seeking solace from *A Course in Miracles.* Written by psychologist Helen Schucman between 1965 and 1972, the Course advances the theory that salvation is achieved by abandoning our ego's stories about who we are. The basic premise, that only love is real and that the opposite of love is fear, resonated with me.

Miracles, we're told, are simply a shift in perception from fear to love. The greatest "miracle" is simply the act of gaining a "full awareness of love's presence" in your life. I began reading a passage from the book every morning before I went to work and was struck by these words: *Nothing real can be threatened. Nothing unreal exists. Herein lies the peace of God.*

Author and motivational speaker Marianne Williamson describes the course as a "self-study program of spiritual psychotherapy." Her first book, *A Return to Love: Reflections on the Principles of a Course in Miracles,* became a bestseller in 1992. I still remember something she said then: *Our deepest fear is that we are powerful beyond measure. It is our light, not our darkness, that most frightens us.*

Like me, Marianne Williamson experienced the "Oprah Effect" after appearing on her show in 1994. To be featured on Oprah's talk show in those days was a career-defining moment for people like us. Remember that it was Oprah who introduced me as "one of the finest colorists in the world," fulfilling a lifelong dream of mine.

Even now I start my day in contemplation, but my practice has expanded to include passages from the Bible and daily devotions from Christian author Joyce Meyer. I've also found comfort in reading anything by Mister Rogers. Published in 2004, the year after he died, *The World According to Mister Rogers: Important Things to Remember* is a collection of wisdom he acquired over the years. I always loved the story he told about the advice his mother gave him for what to do when scary things happen: *Look for the helpers. You will always find people who are helping.*

     Brad Johns with Marianne Dougherty

Fred Rogers was born in Latrobe, Pennsylvania, but he spent most of his life in Pittsburgh where he recorded his television show, *Mister Rogers' Neighborhood*. When I was in grade school, a teacher took us on a field trip to be part of the audience. Being so close to the man I revered, I noticed that he bit his nails. The observation spoiled my notion, naïve at best, that he was perfect, but my mother assured me that no one is perfect, not even Mister Rogers. Since then, I have learned that Fred Rogers was bullied as a child and also suffered from depression just like me. He wasn't perfect, just human like the rest of us, and maybe he bit his nails to deal with his feelings of anxiety and apprehension.

I discovered Eckhart Tolle in 2005 when I read his book, *The New Earth: Awakening to Your Life's Purpose*. I was not surprised when it became an Oprah's Book Club selection. Oprah called it a "wake-up call for the entire planet." It was certainly a wake-up call for me. His teachings mention the awakening state of consciousness, which transcends ego. This awakening, he suggests, is the essential next step in human evolution. The premise is simple: by living in the present moment, we can find "the freedom and joy of life," which is not unlike the tenets of Buddhism.

Sometimes we grasp these concepts intellectually, but your soul has to internalize them. You either do the work in this lifetime or you'll do it in the next. Some people may never do it, stumbling from one lifetime to the next living in fear. It's your choice. One thing I've learned is that love is all encompassing and that I feel God's presence in my life each time I choose love over fear.

– **24** –

Most of us are familiar with the concept of the inner child, the part of our subconscious that retains every meaningful event from our past, good and bad, yet remains hopeful. I met my inner child at a destination spa nestled in the red rocks of Boynton Canyon in Sedona, Arizona. I call him Little B.

Therapists suggest that your inner child is your essence and that it's naturally innocent and fun-loving. That sounds about right since Little B began appearing to me in a cowboy hat. I had gone to Sedona because I was curious about its vortexes, each one radiating energy said to help with healing. Plagued by stomach problems since childhood, I hoped to find relief at Mii Amo Spa, which is located in what has been described as the most beautiful box canyon in Sedona.

What is unique about the Boynton Canyon vortex is that it's a mix of both masculine and feminine energy. While no-nonsense masculine energy is said to encourage self-discipline and self-confidence, the energy of the divine feminine helps you release negative patterns and find forgiveness so you can return to harmony with your true self.

Think of vortexes as concentrated fields of energy that exist along the Earth's power lines. When those lines crisscross, like they do at the Great Pyramids as well as Stonehenge, you get a vortex. There are seven main vortex sites in Sedona, which Native American tribes regarded as the birthplace of their spirituality.

People have gone to Sedona for years to experience a spiritual awakening so it's fitting that Little B revealed himself to me there. A close friend had introduced me to Genie O'Malley, who pioneered a breathing technique called *I Breathe Life* designed to clear your mind of distractions and replace negative emotions with positive suggestions. The goal is to allow self-love instead of brokenness to be the driver of our life experiences. I am convinced that the practice saved my life during the ten years that I was a practitioner.

It was during one of these sessions in my casita at Mii Amo Spa that I heard a voice shout, "Hey!"

When I opened my eyes, I saw Little B's face for the first time. "Who are you?" I asked him.

"Your emotional center," he replied.

"So, why are you here?"

"Because you haven't been listening to me." He went on to explain that my stomachaches were wakeup calls from him. "You have had four hernias from working out too hard, but you kept pushing yourself. Who do you think gave you those hernias?" He gave me a minute before answering his own question. "I had to do something to get your attention."

It didn't take long to realize that Little B was on a mission to coax me into leaving New York and moving to the West Coast. Now that we are here, he is finally at rest, and he sleeps on my shoulder most of the time.

When he first appeared to me, Little B was nothing more than a disembodied face as evanescent as a soap bubble. Over time he became fleshed out, growing arms and legs. Frankly, he looks a lot like I did when I was six years old.

Not long ago I found a picture of myself at that age. My hair is cropped close, what barbers used to call a brush cut, and I am wearing a striped T-shirt and shorts. My expression is pure and unaffected. I chose to use that image on the cover of this book as a reminder that the little boy in that photograph still lives inside me.

     Brad Johns with Marianne Dougherty

— **25** —

hari Marilyn Johns, my baby sister, was born in 1961, and even now I become emotional when I tell her story. Life has never been easy for Shari. Our mother thought she was a mistake. She wasn't a mistake. She has been as a gift to our family since the day she was born, and I don't know how I'd live without her.

When she was little, Shari desperately wanted to take ballet lessons, but my parents couldn't afford them. What she got was the next-best thing: a tutu that she wore to dance around the house, pretending to be a ballerina. When she was around eight or nine, Shari started putting on weight, but none of us understood why. Then, at 18, she got a phone call from our uncle Kenny.

"Remember what we used to do when you were little?" he said. "Why don't we start doing that again? People did this all the time in ancient Rome."

With those words, it all came back in a rush: the pedophilia that went on for years and always at my grandmother's house where Kenny lived. That's when food, like pills for me, became Shari's drug of choice for dealing with the pain.

Worrying that she might be mistaken, that perhaps she had imagined the things that happened in that upstairs bedroom all those years ago, Shari called a therapist she had been seeing for depression.

After Shari provided a few details, the therapist told her

to hang up and call our mother at work. "Tell her what he did to you when you were a little girl."

To her credit, my mother never doubted the veracity of Shari's story. "All my life I protected my kids against the bullies in the schoolyard," she told her brother when she confronted him, "but little did I know there was one in my own family abusing my daughter."

The news tore our family apart. My uncle was my god-father, but after Shari's revelation I hated him. I could not understand how someone who had been a handsome, talented artist could have done something like that to an innocent little girl.

Shari is the purest soul I've ever known, and I've learned so much about empathy and forgiveness from her. At the end of his life, Shari forgave my uncle Kenny for what he'd done to her, preferring to remember the little boy who had been abused himself instead of the damaged person he had become.

My sister showed the same kind of compassion toward my mother, who had beaten her when she stayed out past her curfew in high school. Craig and I felt helpless to stop the abuse when she'd tear into Shari, screaming, "I won't have a whore for a daughter!"

I call Shari the "Angel of Death" because she's the one who ushers the living into the next world when it's their time to go. She was with my father at the end of his life, and she visited our grandmother in the nursing home until she died. When my mother was dying of cancer, Shari was there for her, too.

"I told them that we love them and it's okay to let go," she explained when I asked her what she said to each of them before they died.

     Brad Johns with Marianne Dougherty

My sister is a survivor, and spiritually she is on a whole other plane. In 2004, after enduring debilitating pain her doctor attributed to migraines, she was diagnosed with a brain tumor. My brother found her unconscious on the floor of the bathroom one day, and tests confirmed that her brain had filled with fluid that required multiple procedures to drain. The prognosis was grim, and while the neurosurgeon cautioned that this kind of delicate surgery could result in paralysis or, worse yet, death, Shari was unafraid.

"*Que sera sera*," she told the surgeon. "Let's go!"

When my mother called to tell me that Shari was in the hospital, I came home for the weekend, but I couldn't stay for the surgery because I had forty clients on the books the next day. While I was frantic as I watched her being wheeled into the operating room, Shari was at peace.

"Don't worry, Bert," she called over her shoulder. "I'll be okay." Bert is her nickname for me, a riff on Bertha, the name of one of our beloved babysitters.

On the flight to New York that night, I prayed that God would spare my sister. I had already decided that I wasn't going to bargain with Him, promising to do such-and-such for someone if Shari lived, and I expected nothing short of a complete recovery. The next afternoon when my mother finally called, she told me that Shari had come through the surgery without a hitch and was sitting up in bed eating spaghetti. My prayers had been answered, though Shari had never doubted that they would be.

When I opened my own salon, I hired Shari to be my booker. I thought we'd get to spend more time together, but I was so busy that we barely saw each other. Her favorite flower is lily of the valley, which grows wild in Pennsylvania.

"I'd like to see them again," she said when she told me she was moving back home, "and the squirrels."

I'd kept that luxury apartment in Gateway Towers that I bought with Clairol money, and I told Shari to move in after my parents passed away. Because I know how much she loves cats, I encouraged her to get a kitten, but she never did. I suspect my sister was simply tired of taking care of things that die.

     Brad Johns with Marianne Dougherty

26

t's been my experience that when it's time for a change, the universe starts sending you subtle messages. It's up to you whether to listen or not. I had been living in New York for forty years, had a successful career and owned an apartment in a historic building in the West Village. Important clients invited me to their houses in the Hamptons or to the theater where we had front-row seats to sold-out plays. What's more, I finally had enough money to afford a lifestyle as far removed from OVA as Venus is from Neptune.

The only problem? I wasn't happy. Maybe restless is a better word to describe how I felt. I had survived the infestation of bedbugs that plagued the city and required me to strip off my clothing and throw everything into the washing machine as soon as I got home if I'd been to a movie or out to dinner. I needed antidepressants to make it through the winter. On rainy days it was impossible to get a cab, and there were rats as big as gophers in the subway. I had fallen in love with New York City when it was a fresh-faced ingenue, but she had become an aging film star without me noticing.

Over the past decade or so, I had inched my way down the street from Avon at 725 Fifth Avenue to Elizabeth Arden at 689 Fifth Avenue and now to Saks at 611 Fifth Avenue where my team took up residence at the in-store salon, just steps away from St. Patrick's Cathedral. Talk about a spiritual journey.

The name Saks Fifth Avenue had always been synonymous with status and prestige, and I loved working there. The location was less than ideal for some people, and more than one beauty editor told me that she couldn't see me, or write about me, as long as I was working in the basement. Here's a secret not many people know: Hairdressers love space, and that salon had plenty of it. For once Chris had a space of his own to cut hair, and I had ten chairs, which were occupied at all times.

My celebrity clients had no problem going to the basement to see me. I swear Kristen Johnston was in every ten minutes telling me, "I've gotta be blonder."

What I wanted to create in that space was the kind of relaxed, casual atmosphere you'd find at a neighborhood salon in a small town. One afternoon Matthew Modine came in for color, and I sat him next to a friend of mine from Pittsburgh where Matthew had just filmed *The Dark Knight Rises*. The two of them, both in foils, struck up a conversation. I'm not sure if that would have happened in a *chichi* salon with a better view.

If I had been getting subtle messages from the universe, a hurricane gathering force in the Caribbean was like getting a letter marked *Special Delivery*. On August 21, 2011, a destructive tropical cyclone battered the East Coast, making landfall on the Caribbean island of St. Croix before moving up the coast toward Coney Island. Officially the first hurricane of the season, the World Meteorological Organization named it Irene.

A storm surge pushed the sea level up to four feet above normal in the Battery on the southern tip of Manhattan, increasing the risk of widespread flooding in Lower Manhattan. The city's two airports and the

     Brad Johns with Marianne Dougherty

Holland Tunnel were closed and subways stopped running, an unprecedented event. Thousands of people lost power, and one hundred shelters were set up to house evacuees. The city had not seen anything like Irene since 1821 when a hurricane flooded all of Manhattan south of Canal Street.

When all was said and done, Irene was one of the costliest storms in New York history, resulting in $296 million in damage. I know how lucky I was simply because I was able to stay in my apartment. The landmark building on a tree-lined cobblestone street had been a six-story brick warehouse in 1905. Then in the 1970s, the space was converted into lofts. Now as gale-force winds howled outside, I sat in my living room watching water pour down the walls from the upstairs apartment. It cost me $20,000 to repair the damage.

Again, I heard God's voice whispering in my ear: *Your walls are crying. Maybe it's time to go.* So, for the first time I began to imagine a different life for myself even if that meant picking up and starting all over again someplace else. Maybe that's what the pioneers felt like when they hitched up their Conestoga wagons to a team of horses and headed west. I'd come to New York City because of Laura Nyro. Now it was Joni Mitchell whose siren call I heard: *But my heart cried out for you, California.*

It took me another seven years to work up the courage to leave, moving from one salon to the other after Saks was sold. For about six months I worked for Sharon Dorram, a gifted colorist whose work I admired. Our aesthetics were completely different. I was doing bolder chunks, while she was doing fine highlights. As artists, we were like Picasso and Matisse, but I respected her.

In 2018, I started going to California once a month just to see how I liked it. At first, I stayed at the Mondrian Hotel on the Sunset Strip. Finally, Cindy Sherman asked me why I didn't just rent an apartment since I was spending so much time in Los Angeles. The poor kid who still lived inside me rejected the idea at first. *We don't have that kind of money.* The truth is, we did have that kind of money. So, I started looking for a place. I had a realtor take me to see apartments in Santa Monica, Beverly Hills, Venice. Nothing appealed to me. Finally, we pulled up in front of a building near the Sunset Strip in West Hollywood.

By then, I was tired of looking at real estate every time I came out to Los Angeles. "If this apartment isn't the one for me, I'm going to live in a hotel," I told my broker as we went upstairs.

I had brought my friend Lena, who's a medium, with me. "Your mother's here," she said when we crossed the threshold. "I sense her presence."

I loved my mother, but I didn't necessarily want to live with her. I set those reservations aside as soon as I saw the master bedroom. Walking through the doorway felt like coming home.

When I signed the lease, I knew I'd want a decorator to do a makeover worthy of *Architectural Digest*. That would cost real money though, but I knew it wouldn't be a problem if I sold some of the art that I'd been collecting over the years.

When I asked Cindy if she'd be offended if I sold a couple pieces she'd given me, she waved one hand dismissively. "Go ahead, sell them. I just want you to be happy, and if this makes you happy, I'm all for it."

My apartment on Perry Street in Manhattan was very austere, a bit cold. The apartment in Los Angeles has a completely different vibe. It feels like a real home with lots of cactuses in pots and huge chunks of selenite, a crystal that vibrates at a very fine vibration level. I have always hated throws, but I have a lot of them in this place—draped over the back of the sofa, at the foot of a bed. They look like animal skins, but they're all synthetic. I had stopped eating meat in 1978, but I hadn't been able to give up leather. I wore head-to-toe leather to the clubs, bought leather shoes at Ian's and had a leather sofa in my apartment. You won't find a single animal fiber in this apartment. No down comforters or feather pillows.

For a time, I kept working, going back and forth from Los Angeles to New York where I'd kept my apartment as a lifeline. In retrospect, it was like a man with a wife and mistress who wants to keep his options open.

My longtime assistant Ivy is a gifted colorist, and I knew my clients would be in good hands if I retired. So, why couldn't I let go? It was complicated, and I wrestled with the pros and cons for months. My profession had lifted me out of poverty and enabled me to take care of my family. Being a colorist had been my identity for nearly four decades. Who would I be if I wasn't doing hair? So, I vacillated for a long time, agonizing over the decision. I think God got tired of hearing me ask him what to do.

Then one evening when I was deep in prayer at my apartment on Perry Street, something compelled me to open my eyes. "Wait a minute," I said out loud. "Are you really God or who are you?" For all I knew, I might have been talking to Lucifer or some other dark force that did not have my best interests at heart.

There was a long pause. Then I heard His voice: *It is I, my son.* It was very Old Testament, something right out of the Bible. Moses on Mount Sinai. Samuel heard the voice of God, but he didn't recognize it as such until he received instruction from Eli (Samuel 3: 1-10). Gideon had a similar experience, but he asked for a sign, not once but three times (Judges 6:17-22, 36-40).

I didn't need a sign. I knew what I'd heard, and I made a leap of faith. First, I told my clients that I was retiring but that Ivy would take good care of them. Then I heard God's voice again, only this time there was a sense of urgency to his message: *Sell your apartment before Christmas.* I called my real estate agent and told him to get what he could for my place and wrap up the deal by the end of December.

Two months later we were in the midst of a global pandemic and the country was in lockdown. New York City had become the epicenter of Covid-19, and people were fleeing in droves. There is no way I would have sold my apartment if I'd waited any longer. What's more, I would have had to pay rent in Los Angeles and condo fees on an empty apartment in New York.

I felt an incredible sense of relief, though it was short-lived. God had begun talking to me on a regular basis now, and what he told me was hard to hear: *You're a tyrant, you're a big mouth, and you're a narcissist. Those qualities may have served you while you were in New York, but what are you planning to do with them out here?*

He was right. I didn't like who I was when I lived in New York. I was bossy and opinionated, and I was often unkind to people for no reason at all. I had pushed boyfriends away and not been intimate with anyone. Raul had loved me before I was a famous colorist, but I had been too ambitious to go to Puerto Rico and build a life with him. Now I was filled with regret.

What God demanded of me was forty days spent in his presence. That's the only way I can describe it. They were the most excruciating forty days of my life, but they were also the most rewarding, and when they came to an end, I was reborn.

27

akeovers are powerful. They instill confidence in people who have forgotten who they are, but the big reveal is more than just a physical transformation. I did a lot of makeovers during my career, both on television and in print, and my goal was always to release the joyful, exuberant spirit that dwelled inside each and every one of the women who sat in my chair.

Now God was telling me that it was time for my makeover, though this one would require me to dredge up painful memories I'd tried to repress with drugs or sex or work. What if I crashed and fell? That was my biggest fear, but God had assured me that he'd be with me on this journey, and I had to surrender to his will. As it turned out, it took a whole year for me to learn to trust God enough to do the work that would be necessary if I wanted to find the peace that had eluded me for so long.

Before selling my apartment and severing all ties to my former life in New York, and before the pandemic forced us all into isolation, I lived the unexamined life Socrates warned us about. A half dozen of my friends had left New York and were already living in Los Angeles when I got here. We partied every night, going out for dinner before hitting the gay bars in West Hollywood or coming back to my apartment where we smoked marijuana or drank margaritas or tequila well into the wee hours of the morning.

    Brad Johns with Marianne Dougherty

Most nights I didn't go to sleep until five a.m. It was like I'd never left New York, and I was still the same person I had been when I lived there: an overbearing know-it-all offering officious opinions about everything. I believe I tossed the word *loathe* around frequently to describe some celebrity I couldn't stand. My friends only tolerated my bad behavior because they'd gotten used to it. Then came the reckoning.

Christmas has always been my favorite holiday. When we were on public assistance, there never seemed to be enough money, but we always got everything we asked for at Christmas. Each summer my mother had us make a list of toys we wanted, and sure enough every toy on that list was under the tree when we came downstairs on Christmas morning. Years later I learned that my mother had put everything on layaway and made installment payments each month so we wouldn't be disappointed.

It was our tradition to have Christmas dinner at my grandmother's house: ham, turkey with stuffing, mashed potatoes, jellied cranberry sauce, carrots and sweet corn and homemade rolls. For dessert there were nut rolls with apple and cinnamon filling and fried dough dipped in powdered sugar. The house was so warm and inviting when we arrived in our winter coats and hats, and there were always presents under the tree, which my grandmother paid for with S&H Green Stamps. Supermarkets used to give them out at the checkout counter, and she redeemed them for gifts that we had seen in the catalog.

After I moved to New York, Christmas was never the same. I came home to celebrate the holiday with my family, but I spent a lot of time partying with my friends. We all drank too much and did way too many drugs. One year I brought a boyfriend home to Pittsburgh with me, but all

I remember about that trip is going to a disco downtown high on cocaine and Ecstasy.

Now here I was living in Los Angeles, presumably older and wiser, and what I wanted to do that first Christmas was have dinner on Christmas Eve with a few close friends and my sister, who had come to visit. We ate at The Henry, a beautiful new restaurant in West Hollywood with a timeless vibe, an eclectic menu and a great wine list. Surrounded by this group of loving, caring people brought back memories of my childhood when my mother and my grandmother did everything in their power to give us a Christmas that made us feel rich. It wasn't just the abundance of toys under the tree but how it felt to gather around the table with all of these people whose blood runs in your veins. My family wasn't perfect, but I knew they loved me.

After dinner at The Henry that night, we all went outside where fairy lights twinkled in the trees. Everyone was taking photos so we'd remember my first Christmas in Los Angeles. A year later Shari was the only person in those photos who was still talking to me. I'd had a falling out with a lot of people by then for reasons I can barely remember now, but it would get a lot worse before it got better.

I had always loved spending time in art galleries or museums, and I was excited that I had a whole new world to explore now that I lived in Los Angeles. The Broad, an art museum downtown near the Walt Disney Concert Hall, houses an impressive collection of contemporary art by artists like Robert Rauschenberg, Jeff Koons, Jean-Michel Basquiat, Andy Warhol and my friend Cindy Sherman. I'd visited the Getty Villa in Pacific Palisades along the Malibu coast, the Museum of Contemporary Art (MOCA) that focuses on nothing but art from 1940 to the present and the

Los Angeles County Museum of Art (LACMA), the largest museum in the western United States.

While I'm partial to contemporary art, I drove to Pasadena to see the vast collection of Impressionist and Post-Impressionist paintings at the Norton Simon Museum. That visit brought back memories of my friend Jeff and our trips to the Carnegie Museum of Art in Pittsburgh all those years ago.

During my first year in Los Angeles, I was never at a loss for things to do, but then came the lockdown. Not only were museums and art galleries closed, so were movie theaters, restaurants and shops where I engaged in retail therapy whenever I was lonely or depressed. I had bought tickets for my first concert at the Hollywood Bowl, but when they canceled the whole season, I donated the money to Covid relief. I'd seen *Light in the Piazza* at the Dorothy Chandler Pavilion twice, but now I imagined it would be a long time before actors would return to the stage.

If I had been reluctant to spend forty days with God, whatever that meant, the pandemic gave me no choice. The sense of isolation was crippling, and I woke up every morning in abject despair, the six-year-old me again who was afraid to leave the bedroom because the bullies would beat me up and rip my clothes on the way to school. The thing my mother feared most was being trapped. Now I was living her worst nightmare, though trapped by a pandemic, not an unhappy marriage. I had most of my meals delivered, but on occasion I ventured out in an N95 mask to pick up a few groceries at Gelson's Market. Like everyone else, I binge-watched shows on Netflix while eating junk food to deal with the relentless boredom and put on weight.

I worried that I'd die and no one would find my body for weeks. Who cared about me now that I'd pushed every-one away? Most of my friends from New York had moved elsewhere: back to New York or to Seattle or Michigan or Mexico. One of them called to say that they had all been afraid of me.

"Do you know how tyrannical you are?" he asked.

Until that moment, I'd had no idea. Then, alone in my apartment with nothing to distract me from the truth, I faced facts.

I had created a world in which no one ever got close to me. I'd been a sensitive child, but I made a conscious decision to harden myself so I could focus on work and make enough money to support my family. That was my job, wasn't it? At least I thought it was. I also had a very precise set of rules for everything, and I expected everyone to follow them. It was my way or the highway.

My New York apartment was devoid of clutter or any-thing that offered a clue as to who I really was. I doubt that anyone felt comfortable there. I'd overheard someone tell his sister when they came to visit, "Brad is very neat. Don't throw anything in the garbage can. There's nothing in there."

Now alone in my penthouse apartment, the city as quiet as it would ever be, the freeways nearly empty, I started crying all the time, which was new for me. I hadn't cried since I was a little boy, but now I was sobbing so hard that one of my neighbors came to the door to see if everything was all right.

I had started arguments with everyone who ever meant anything to me, except for my sister, and now they were all gone. I guess they were fed up. All that was left to do was climb up on the cross and suffer the consequences. So, I asked God to tell me what to do, and he answered almost immediately: *You need to learn how to be patient. Patient with yourself and with others. Stop being critical of everyone. Learn forgiveness.*

One day God told me to put $20 in my pocket. "Why?" I asked foolishly. Long pause. *Go for a walk. You'll know what to do.* So, fully masked and wearing Latex gloves, I left the apartment and walked up to Sunset Boulevard where I saw a homeless man in front of the drugstore. I pulled the twenty out of my pocket and offered it to him. My old self, the cynical New Yorker, decided that he'd probably spend it on liquor or drugs, but the person God wanted me to become came to another conclusion: *It's not your business what he does with the money. You did what God asked you to do, and now it's up to him.*

As I walked away, I saw him heading toward McDonald's, and I broke down. I had enough money to eat at the finest restaurants in Los Angeles where I dropped $100 on a bottle of wine and ordered more food than I could eat, while this man was grateful simply because I'd given him enough money to eat at a fast-food restaurant. What had my mother told me when I was growing up? *Life isn't fair.* Maybe it isn't, but I had the wherewithal to even the playing field a little. Maybe that's what God wanted me to understand.

The next morning God told me to go to the ATM and withdraw a few hundred dollars. I knew better than to argue with him, and for weeks I walked around handing out money to anyone who looked like they needed it more than I did. One day I saw a Black woman pushing a shopping cart loaded with all of her earthly possessions. She was singing some old Motown hit like one of The Supremes.

"Could you use this?" I asked her.

She took the fifty from me and hollered, "Thank you, baby Jesus!" Then, regarding me thoughtfully, she added, "Thank you brother."

That's when I realized that it doesn't matter what race, what gender, what sexual orientation you are. We are all God's children, and we are responsible for one another.

After a few weeks of that, God upped the ante. He didn't even wait until I threw back the covers before prodding me into action. *You know who you need to send money to today?*

He didn't wait for an answer but rattled off a name, often someone I'd stopped talking to for one reason or another. The next morning it was someone else. I paid rent for old friends who were out of work. I sent checks to people I hadn't seen in years. The pandemic was harder for some people than others, people who had no savings or lived paycheck to paycheck. I sent money to all of them.

After those forty days with God, I began making phone calls. I apologized to everyone I'd hurt, and to their credit each of them forgave me. Now what I needed to do was learn how to forgive myself, which is a lot more difficult.

Those months I spent in contemplation taught me a valuable lesson: how to live in the moment. I see a therapist once a week, and I walk the ten long blocks to his office from my apartment. On the way I stop to admire the beauty all around me. I hug trees now, literally put my arms around the trunks of ancient figs whose roots have crawled up through the soil to spill out onto the pavement. Trees have been powerful symbols of growth and resurrection for centuries. Taoists believe that trees radiate with subtle energy. Wrap your arms around a tree and you'll feel it.

The weather in New York and in Pittsburgh where I grew up is dismal much of the time with lots of cold, gray days

     Brad Johns with Marianne Dougherty

and overcast skies. In California the sky is nearly always a brilliant shade of bottle-blue, and there are bursts of color to be found everywhere. The sheer amount of plant life is staggering. The state flower of California is the poppy. Also known as the flame flower, it's a beautiful shade of orange. Indigenous communities used the petals of the pale purple Douglas Iris to weave fishing nets and ropes. Indian Paintbrush blooms in spring and holds onto its bright coral color throughout summer. If you drive north to Santa Ynez from late February to early May, you'll pass fields of bright orange poppies and purple lupine.

The flowers you see here are remarkably adaptable. Redwood Sorel has evolved to thrive in the shade and will actually bow toward the ground in direct sunlight, its leaves opening again once the shade returns. Other plants and flowers have learned to tolerate salt and grow in profusion at the beach: rosemary, English ivy, geraniums, sea buckthorn. By adapting to change, these plants have thrived in a hostile environment. It's something I think about when life throws me a curveball.

Along my walks, I've stopped to admire flowers growing in someone's garden. One woman has the prettiest roses I've ever seen. Ramtha believed that the correct way to smell a rose so that you get its essence is to bury your nose deep in the center and inhale deeply. I do that now, and I've discovered that a white rose has a different scent from an orange rose or a red rose. Some people jog by without noticing the flowers at all. Others are looking down at their phones as they pass me on the street. I literally stop and smell the roses.

28

had been living in Los Angeles for less than a year when my aunt Alice died of renal failure. The date is easy to remember because it was a holiday: June 14, 2018. Flag Day. My cousin Lynn asked me to speak at the funeral, but I couldn't bring myself to do it. I knew I'd ugly cry if I stood up there in front of all those people and tried to explain how much her mother had meant to me.

Alice taught me about fashion. "Look sharp," was one of her commandments. "Buy a few good pieces you can mix and match and wear for years," was another. It was Alice who took me to the Jersey Shore and showed me that there was a whole world beyond Pittsburgh and OVA.

The funeral mass was held at Mother of Sorrows where Alice had taken me to mass in that long ago life so I'd have at least a passing relationship with God. She had been young and beautiful then, daring anyone to judge her for flaunting her good looks and inherent instinct for fashion. I used to tell editors, "Natural isn't the point. Fabulous is the point." I learned that from Alice.

One of the last times I saw my aunt Alice was the summer before she died. I had used some of my Clairol money to buy her a modest ranch house with three bedrooms on Palace Avenue in McKees Rocks. After it was remodeled, Alice called it her palace.

Now, sitting on her front porch, she told me how lonely

     Brad Johns with Marianne Dougherty

she was. "There's no one who remembers what it was like to go downtown to listen to jazz at one of the supper clubs," she said. "I can't talk to anyone about World War II or anything else that happened before they were born."

For the most part, the men in my family were either weak or abusive. It was the women who exuded strength: my grandmother, my mother and my aunt Alice. No wonder I made it my life's work to make women feel beautiful.

Like other women of their era, my grandmother and both of her daughters had few opportunities outside of marriage and motherhood. My grandmother was really smart, but she gave up her dream of becoming a lawyer when she became pregnant with my mother and dropped out of school to marry my grandfather. I know my own mother felt trapped at home with three kids when she had so much more to offer, and she was angry with me when I referred to her as a homemaker in *People* magazine.

"I worked for HUD," she reminded me. "I worked for VISTA."

Maybe that's why they imagined a bigger life for me. Still, while my grandmother's support was unwavering, my mother was harder to please. Nothing was ever good enough for her. Years ago, she told me that if I were really rich, I wouldn't have to work anymore. While those words still sting, I would have done anything for my mother, who probably battled more demons that I have.

All three of them, who I call my *sacred feminine*, are gone now, but there are still three women in my life who are happy to fill in for them: Shari, Lynn and Vivian. How lucky am I?

For a long time after she died, my mother sat at the edge of my bed each morning. She appeared blurry and indistinct, a photograph that's out of focus. I may not see my aunt Alice, but I sense her presence all the time. One day I noticed that my cactuses weren't looking so good, and I heard Alice's voice: *Water them.* I knew that cactuses were succulents that stored water in their roots and that overwatering could kill them, but I had always gone to Alice for practical advice so I did what I was told. She still tells me when it's time to water my cactuses, which are thriving by the way.

I guess what I'm trying to say is that I take advice from people now, I listen closely to what they have to tell me. I used to be a big mouth, a know-it-all. I think I've mentioned that before. Through God, I've learned to be humble.

My mother was a deeply flawed human being, but protected me from the bullies who called me a fairy when I was growing up in OVA. She came to my defense more than once when I was laughed at by the neighborhood kids for something as trivial as piercing my ears. My being gay was never an issue for her either, and for that I am grateful.

My grandmother taught me to be thrifty, and she appreciated every gift I ever gave her. One Christmas I bought her a jar of potpourri made from dried flower petals and essential oils. She told me how much she loved the scent, but when my mother pointed out how much money I'd spent, she had a fit. "Don't ever buy me anything that expensive again," she said, as if I'd listen. I would have done anything for her.

Before my uncle Kenny died, he told Alice that he was sorry for what he had done to Shari when she was a little girl.

"You need to tell Shari, not me," Alice told him, but Kenny shook his head. "I can't." Like I said, the men in my family were either weak or abusive. It was the "sacred feminine" from which I drew my strength.

     Brad Johns with Marianne Dougherty

29

For hairdressers who achieve the level of success I did, keeping up appearances is part of the job description. At the height of my fame, I had publicity photos taken by some of the most famous photographers in the world, including Francesco Scavullo, and my high-end clientele included the most beautiful and powerful women in New York. Because I suspected that they would not want to have their hair done by an aging queen with sagging jowls and undereye bags, I knew that cosmetic surgery was probably in my future.

Dorian Gray, the fictional protagonist of Oscar Wilde's novel, exchanges his soul for eternal youth. Fortunately, I didn't have to go that far. I had Dr. Daniel Baker, a true artist, though his medium was flesh. On my first visit to his office, Dr. Baker was very specific about the limitations of his craft.

"One thing I can't do is make you look seventeen again," he told me. Instead, the idea was to make it appear that I had just returned from a long, relaxing vacation.

A couple of years went by before I noticed that I was developing a pouch of fat under my chin. I asked Dr. Baker if he could remove it. He could, and he did. A few more years passed, and I asked him if it was time for a facelift. Having abused barbiturates for so many years, my skin lacked elasticity.

"Not yet," he said, "but we can do a little something."

You have to realize that I spent all day in front of a mirror. When I didn't like what I saw, I did something about it: a little Botox, a little lipo, eventually a full facelift. When a beauty editor asked Kenneth, the famed hairdresser who had given Jackie Kennedy her iconic bob, to comment on my penchant for plastic surgery, which was certainly no secret to anyone who knew me, he suggested that I was trying to look like Lee Radziwill.

When his remarks appeared in print, a number of editors called to ask for my reaction. If they were expecting me to be offended, they were disappointed because I would have loved to look like Jackie Kennedy's younger sister, who was a great beauty.

Now that I don't see clients anymore, I no longer feel the need for the occasional nip or tuck. I've accepted the fact that I'm getting older, and I generally like what I see when I look in the mirror: a 68-year-old man who doesn't look his age but doesn't look like he wants to be seventeen again either.

One day when I was sitting outside on my patio, I noticed that the skin on my arms was beginning to look like crepe paper. The realization was mildly disconcerting since I tend to wear sleeveless T-shirts year-round now that I live in a temperate climate. Despite the fact that Oribe had sleeves of tattoos, the idea never appealed to me. Now I thought about using my flesh as a canvas to draw attention away from my crepey skin.

My first tattoo was actually a series of crosses. Since three is my sacred number, there are a trio of them. The large cross on my left wrist symbolizes Jesus Christ, while the other two represent Dismas and Gestas, the two

     Brad Johns with Marianne Dougherty

thieves who were crucified alongside him. The cross on my right wrist is for Dismas, who proclaimed Christ's innocence and asked to be remembered when he came into his kingdom. The small cross beneath my left eye is for Gestas, the unrepentant thief who dared Jesus to prove that he was the Messiah by saving himself. Unlike Dismis, who placed his hope in the next world, Gestas lost the opportunity for salvation by placing his faith in this world. His cross is the only tattoo on my face because it sends a powerful message.

When I went in for my second tattoo, I decided on a phrase from the Bible that has helped me put my childhood into perspective: *Forgive them for they know not what they do.* For me, forgiveness is the key to salvation, and I have worked hard to see the good, not the bad, in people who let me down when I was growing up.

The words *que sera sera* (whatever will be will be) are tattooed in script on my left arm. In the 1950s, Doris Day had a hit with the song "Que Sera Sera," and those are the words Shari said to me as she was being wheeled into the operating room for brain surgery. My sister is the bravest person I've ever known, and that day her faith was strong enough to accept the outcome of her surgery, good or bad.

I've also chosen to honor other members of my family. The letters *pcj* are my father's initials. *GTA* is for my sacred feminine: Grace (my grandmother), Thelma (my mother) and Alice. For Craig, I chose the words from a song by The Hollies: *he ain't heavy, he's my brother.* The letters *JRC*, each in a different color, are for my cousin Chris and his sons, Julian and Raphael.

The word *contigo* is for Raul, the love of my life. It was his favorite song.

As my tattoos proliferated, it became clear that my flesh was becoming a living message board for the people, songs and beliefs that have shaped me. Lyrics from "Moon River" are a nod to my long friendship with Vivian: *two drifters off to see the world, there's such a lot of world to see.* Lyrics from a Todd Rundgren song will resonate for anyone who's ever contemplated suicide: *hope i'm around.* From a Barbara Mason song I've always loved are the words *yes, i'm ready.* That's how I felt every time I started a new relationship. It's how I feel now about the future I imagine with a loving partner someday. On the underside of one arm is a line from Barbra Streisand's "Yentl" that means a lot to me: *to see myself, to free myself, to be myself.* Those words are significant because I feel like I've finally arrived at a place where I actually see myself and have freed myself to be myself. There's this from the back of a Laura Nyro album: *where is the night luster past my trials,* and the lyrics *to your fingertips to the summer sunset.* And on my forearm *ELI AND THE THIRTEENTH CONFESSION.*

I have very few images on my arms: a mouse for my former assistant Ivy (I called her Little Mouse); a ladybug for Shari because my nickname for her is Tootlebug; a peace sign for my cousin Lynn; a book with a blue cover for my co-author Marianne Dougherty; and a scorpion (my astrological sign is Scorpio) that was painted by her grandson, Levi, who is on the spectrum and a gifted artist since childhood. Tattooing his art on my arm was my way of telling him how much I believe in him.

Without faith, I don't think I'd still be here, so on my left arm are the words I AM YOUR KINGDOM. On my right arm: I AM SUSTAINED BY THE LOVE OF GOD. On the wrist I would have sliced had I taken my own life is *THIS*

     Brad Johns with Marianne Dougherty

TOO SHALL PASS. In lowercase on one arm are the words *i rest in god*. On the other: *i trust god*. The circle inside the letter "o" is red for the blood he shed for our sins.

Finally, since I believe that we have the power to manifest our hopes and dreams, the word *DYE*, the name of this book, is inked in all caps on my left arm. If you want to send a message to the universe, put it in writing.

30

Here's the thing about faith. Just because we believe in God doesn't mean that we'll coast through life unscathed. Bad things happen to good people. Rabbi Harold S. Kushner understood that better than anyone. Despite the fact that his faith was strong, his three-year-old son was diagnosed with a degenerative disease that would ultimately take his life. To make sense of it all, he wrote a book, *When Bad Things Happen to Good People*, that has become a bestseller since its publication in 1981.

Nonbelievers might ask, "How could God let that kind of thing happen to a good man and his innocent son?" My faith tells me that God's purpose is not to interfere in our lives here on Earth, saving this person but not that one, curing this person of a terminal illness but not that one. What God can do is walk beside us on our journey, offering comfort and support when we are most afraid. At least that was my experience when I was diagnosed with prostate cancer in 2021.

When you grow up in poverty, you're always waiting for the other shoe to drop. Now that I had finally let go of my fear of being poor again, the other shoe dropped with the force of a bomb exploding.

God had been telling me to see my doctor for a couple of weeks. The first time I heard his voice, I ignored it. I did the same thing the second time he told me to call my doctor.

 Brad Johns with Marianne Dougherty

The third time I heard his voice, he sounded rather peeved with me. "Make an appointment now!" he told me in what I think of as his Old Testament voice: a thunderclap.

So, I made an appointment with my urologist. After the examination, he removed his gloves and said, "We have a problem here."

I hadn't seen that coming. "Now what?" I asked him.

"We schedule a biopsy."

He got me in right away, and after the procedure his nurse told me, "If I call you tomorrow, you're fine. If he calls you, you're not." Then, as if to soften the blow, she added, "Don't worry, Brad, you'll be all right."

The next morning when I answered the phone, it was my doctor on the line, not his nurse. I steeled myself for the news, sorry for not paying attention the first time when God told me to see my doctor. Joyce Meyer always says, "You need to trust God when he talks to you." Why hadn't I listened?

I'm convinced that no one is ever prepared to hear the word cancer. The Big C. Yet I felt surprisingly calm when the doctor informed me that my prostate was riddled with it. "What's my homework?" I asked him.

He gave me a book to read about what to expect after prostate surgery. I have always been able to compartmentalize, and I think that's what I did after I was diagnosed. Little B internalized all of my fear, while I focused on what I needed to do to get through the surgery. I was that little boy in third grade again, diligently memorizing his times tables, only now I was learning everything I could about prostate cancer. Had the cancer spread? Would I have to go through chemo and radiation? Would I be incontinent, which was a common side effect after prostate surgery. So was erectile dysfunction, though that was the least of my problems since I hadn't been seeing anyone and there were no prospects on the horizon.

Both Shari and my cousin Lynn offered to come to Los Angeles to take care of me, but I didn't want to be a burden on anyone. At least that's the excuse I used when I turned them down. The truth is, I am essentially a very private person, and I didn't want anyone to see me like that, whatever that was. I knew I'd come home from the hospital wearing a catheter, and the last thing I wanted was for either of them to be emptying the bag.

Instead, I asked my personal assistant Wendy, who is one of the helpers Mister Rogers talked about, to take me to the hospital the morning of the surgery. It was pitch dark outside and cold even for California in mid-November when we left for Santa Monica. We both knew she wouldn't be able to come in due to Covid restrictions so she dropped me off at the front door.

"Good luck," she said, but I had already left the outcome in God's hands. I'd either live or die. *Que sera sera.*

The surgery took place deep in the bowels of UCLA Santa Monica Medical Center. With robotic-assisted laparoscopic prostate surgery, there's less chance that parts of the malignant tumor will be left behind, and patients typically go home sooner and recover more quickly. My surgeon wasn't even in the room. Instead, he was at a computer console manipulating tiny instruments that offer a far greater range of motion than the human wrist. The anesthesiologist had come into the room to administer a sedative, but even he wasn't allowed to stay.

Before I drifted off into a Propofal-induced coma, I whispered, "God, I'm in your hands."

     Brad Johns with Marianne Dougherty

I had not been allowed to eat solid food for two days before the surgery, and I was starving when I woke up in recovery. At my request, a nurse gave me graham crackers and a glass of Ginger Ale. Since the anesthesia hadn't worn off yet, I wasn't in any pain. That would come later.

I went home with a prescription for Ocycodone and a catheter as big as a garden hose. At least that's what it felt like. The bag that would collect my urine for the next seven days was strapped to my leg. I'm a side sleeper, and I was afraid that I'd roll over during the night and disconnect the whole apparatus. I'd been given instructions on how to empty the bag, which I had to do more frequently than I expected.

I let Little B handle my turbulent emotions (I couldn't let myself cry every time I had to change my own catheter bag) while I methodically pinched the soft rubber catheter tube to keep urine from leaking out, disconnected the urinary catheter tube from the bag with a twisting motion, placed the old bag on a towel, removed the plastic cap from the end of the bag tubing, cleaned the tip with an alcohol pad, inserted the bag tubing tip in the catheter tube and fastened the straps of the new bag to my leg.

During surgery, my doctor had noticed three little spots on my spine that he deemed suspicious. There was some discussion as to whether or not I might need further treatment, and I was waiting to hear from him. I knew I'd be seeing him in a few days to have the catheter removed and hoped I'd know something by then. As much as I trusted God, I'm only human, and I was worried about the prospect of chemo and radiation. I'd known too many people who had died an agonizing death after multiple rounds of chemotherapy.

I still hadn't let any of my friends visit me at home, but a number of them called every day to see how I was doing. One morning I talked to a friend who became alarmed because I seemed out of it and was slurring my words. Her concern was that I might have sepsis, which could cause those symptoms, and would die alone because I had refused to allow a caregiver or anyone else inside my apartment.

While her instinct was to drop in and see for herself if I was in trouble, she lived two hours away. So, she called my sister to see if she'd talked to me that day. Shari and I had spoken earlier that morning, but she promised to call me. What neither of them knew was that I had taken enough pain medication to knock me out cold. I needed sleep so I turned off my cell phone. When Shari couldn't reach me on my cell, she called my landline, but the batteries had died.

Unsure what to do, my friend decided to call 911, which connected her to the sheriff's office in West Hollywood. They sent a couple of law enforcement officers to my apartment to do a wellness check. Meanwhile, Shari called Wendy to ask if she could drive over to my apartment to find out what was going on.

So, here I am in a drug-induced stupor, probably drooling on my pillow, when I hear someone shouting my name and pounding on the front door. I stagger into the living room, the catheter tube trailing from my penis, the bag strapped to my leg like a gunslinger's pistol. There at a bank of windows that overlooks my patio are four young, gorgeous police officers, guns drawn. *Was I dreaming?* They certainly looked like something the Oxy might have conjured up, an aging gay man's fantasy. Then I saw Wendy, who was cowering behind them. I mean, they were armed.

Now I was angry. Since that night I convulsed at Infinity, I had assiduously avoided any kind of run-in with the police, yet here they were. I let them in so they could search the apartment on the off-chance that someone had been holding me hostage in the bedroom. When they were satisfied that I was all right, they left.

Later I realized how lucky I was to have friends who cared enough about me to take drastic measures to ensure that I was all right. The same thing had happened years ago in New York when I'd taken so many Tuinals that I slept for two days. My boyfriend became so worried when he didn't hear from me that he brought a group of friends to my apartment where they broke down the door to see if I was still alive.

A couple of days later, I was still waiting to find out if I'd need chemo or not and my nerves were shot. When I woke up in the middle of the night to change the catheter bag, I decided to do it in the shower so I wouldn't have to clean up the floor if I made a mess. Suddenly there was blood everywhere. Frantic, I stepped out of the shower. When I realized that I'd accidentally disconnected the tubing, I reached for my phone to call an Uber to take me to the hospital.

There is a huge mirror over the vanity in my bathroom, and I could see my reflection in it. Then I heard God's voice: *Would you die for him?* "Die for who?" I asked my own reflection because somehow it was as if God had inhabited my earthly body and was speaking to me through my image in the mirror.

Would you die for him?

I was still struggling to comprehend. "Die for who?"

He rephrased the question. *Will you die for any of my children?"*

After a long pause, he assured me that radiation, if it came to that, would not be easy but that He would be there for me.

When God asked Abraham to take his son Isaac to the region of Moriah and sacrifice him as a burnt offering, he didn't hesitate. I didn't either. "Yes, I'd die for them."

In tears, I told my/God's reflection, "I am sustained by your love." Then it was just my reflection in that mirror again.

The Uber driver asked if everything was okay because I was literally sobbing in the backseat. I told him about my cancer and explained that I was waiting to find out if the nodules on my spine might be malignant. He seemed genuinely concerned.

Then I heard a ping on my phone alerting me that an email had come in. It was from the doctor's office: *Per Doctor Chamie, there is no need for radiation. You are scheduled for your voiding trial and catheter removal tomorrow. Thank you, Jesus.*

I knew full well that Dr. Chamie's assistant pronounces his name HAY-sus, not GEE-sus, but it didn't matter. In that moment God was sending a message to me through His son, Jesus, and no one will ever convince me otherwise.

     Brad Johns with Marianne Dougherty

31

This book is populated by ghosts: family, friends and lovers, whose spirits hover over the keyboard even now. Cancer took a lot of them from me. AIDS took the rest. Oribe's death right before Christmas in 2018 was devastating to those of us who knew him. Handsome and charismatic, Oribe was enough of a celebrity to merit an obituary in *The New York Times* where Christy Turlington remembered driving around Manhattan in Oribe's Jeep, parking in front of some nightclub and watching people go in and out.

I flew to New York from Los Angeles for the memorial at Lincoln Center. Christy was there to eulogize the man who changed all of our lives. Garren said a few words that day, remembering how he'd hired a young Oribe Canales to work at his salon in the Plaza Hotel and convinced him to drop his last name, like Cher or Madonna.

Like me, Oribe had wanted to be an actor before he became a hairdresser. When he was sixteen, he studied acting in Miami. Two years later he moved to Buffalo, New York, where he got his hairdressing license.

I knew I'd have to dress appropriately for the memorial so I packed the black Tom Ford suit I'd bought when he was designing for Gucci. Because no one loved bling as much as Oribe, I put three diamond studs in one ear and a diamond eternity band on my left pinkie for him.

A few of us who had worked for Oribe at his opulent salon on Fifth Avenue slipped into the back row. There were a lot of fashion phonies at the memorial making a big show of how grief-stricken they were, but those of us who really knew Oribe were too sad to cry that day. Ours was the kind of sadness that defies tears.

Oribe was sixty-two when he died of complications from cancer. At sixty-eight, I am a cancer survivor, and for that I am grateful. That's another thing Oribe taught me: to be grateful for everything.

Lately I've been thinking a lot about my boyhood friend Jeff Sevcik, who not only introduced me to art but also took me to The Pittsburgh Playhouse where we saw plays like *Gypsy* or *Company*. When we were 13, we saw *Funny Girl* at the Parkway Theater in McKees Rocks. Our friend John was with us, and I will never forget how he jumped to his feet and burst into thunderous applause as the credits scrolled across the screen.

Growing up in Pittsburgh, Jeff and I were frequently bored. Longing to escape, we'd go to the airport and watch people who had the money to go someplace else. Both of us were fascinated by an Alexander Calder mobile made of aluminum and iron that was suspended from the ceiling, and after learning that it had been exhibited at the 1958 Carnegie International, we decided that we needed to live in a city where people made things like that.

On a trip to Myrtle Beach with our friend Jim while we were still in high school, Jeff tried to kiss me. Pushing him away, I told him that I didn't like him *that way*. Now I wish I'd handled things differently, but I was still coming to terms with my own sexuality.

Years later when we were both living in New York, I visited Jeff at the apartment he shared with his longtime

     Brad Johns with Marianne Dougherty

partner, gay rights advocate Vito Russo. Vito had written *The Celluloid Closet: Homosexuality in the Movies*, and I spent a lot of time with them watching obscure movies he brought home in huge metal canisters. Jeff's favorite movie of all time was *Member of the Wedding*, which was based on the novel by Carson McCullers. The actress Julie Harris starred as Frankie Addams, an awkward, moody tomboy who doesn't fit in. I think Jeff identified with her.

The actress Geraldine Page and her husband, actor Rip Torn, lived in the same building. There was a row of mailboxes in the lobby, and Jeff founded it incredibly funny that the nameplate above their mailbox read TORN/PAGE.

Jeff was only thirty years old when he died of AIDS in March, 1986. Vito called to tell me that Jeff had wanted me to know that I was the person he loved most in this world. I think I cried for a week.

The AIDS Memorial Quilt with 1,920 individual panels, each inscribed with the name of someone who died of AIDS, was displayed on the National Mall in Washington, D.C. for the first time on October 11, 1987. Vito made one of those panels for Jeff, and it's featured along with Jeff's story in the 1989 Academy Award-winning documentary *Common Threads: Stories from the Quilt*. A year later at forty-four, Vito was dead as well from AIDS-related complications.

Why so many people I loved died of AIDS and I didn't has troubled me for years. While I had never been promiscuous and had avoided anonymous sex in the gay baths in New York, I also knew that I had been lucky. Jonathan and I were in what I thought was a monogamous relationship, yet he was sleeping around. The fact that he contracted the disease and didn't pass it on to me is nothing short of a miracle.

Of all the friends and lovers that I lost to AIDS, it's Raul who haunts me the most. Raul taught me how to be gay and proud. He taught me to be human. I often wonder what kind of life we would have had if I'd opened that studio in Puerto Rico like he wanted me to instead of going back to New York to focus on my career. Raul's extended family would have become my family.

I regret those lost years with Raul, but I can't turn back time. Still, if I could pick up the phone and hear his voice, I'd tell him how sorry I am for everything and that I'm grateful that he was able to overlook my flaws and love me unconditionally.

My parents are another story. For most of her childhood, my mother lived in a house owned by her maternal grandparents in a section of McKees Rocks known as the Hollow. Her father, Salvatore Ciccone, worked for the WPA during the Depression. When he was drafted during World War II, he already had a wife and family, and he took them with him when he was deployed to Louisiana.

My mother hated going to school in the South where her dark, ethnic looks set her apart from the other students, remembering that when she walked into the classroom the teacher announced, "Here comes another Yankee."

When she lived at her grandfather's house in the Hollow, my mother had to wash up at the sink. After the war her father was able to buy a little house in McKees Rocks where he installed a shower in the basement. Having an actual shower must have seemed like a step up, but it was still a hardscrabble life.

My father's young life wasn't much better. When he was a teenager, he worked for Weirton Coal Company in the remote coal or "patch town" of Isabella in Fayette County in

          Brad Johns with Marianne Dougherty

southwestern Pennsylvania. It was a kind of planned community that provided mining families with the basic necessities such as housing and medical care. The mine and town were built in 1910 on the banks of the Monongahela River about 45 miles south of Pittsburgh. A section of the Isabella tipple is still in existence today. My father lived about seven miles away in the borough of Brownsville. I am not sure if he owned an automobile or how he made the commute each day, but it must have been a hard life for an 18-year-old boy.

Perhaps enlisting in the Air Force seemed like a way out, and he had served honorably during World War II (Ground Crew/Other Service, Support Units). Records in the National Archives indicate that in October, 1944, he was hospitalized and treated for an unspecified condition and discharged a month later after two years, four months of military service. He was 20 years old.

At the end of her life when she was dying with cancer, I think my mother realized how badly she'd treated my father. When she asked me why he was willing to change her diapers now that she was bedridden, I told her, "Because he's your best friend, and he loves you." I'm not sure if she believed me.

During the five years it took my mother to succumb to breast and bone cancer, I was summoned to Pittsburgh on a number of occasions. Each time she believed that the end was near. One time when I showed up, I found her working in her garden. Now I realize that she just wanted to see me, and I wish I'd gone home more often.

Because I was born on October 27, Halloween was one of my mother's favorite holidays. "You were the only thing I ever did right," she used to tell me, though I'm not sure that's true.

In 2004, I was in Pittsburgh on Halloween when my mother took her last breath. A hospital bed had been set up in the dining room, and we were alone. As always, she looked to me for answers.

"Where am I going?" She seemed frightened.

"You're going home, and I'll meet you there one day," I told her. In that moment, we were not mother and son. We were simply two souls connecting in the most intimate way. Being with my mother as she exited this earthly plane was a deeply moving and profound experience.

After my mother's death, my father seemed lost. I came home one weekend to find him sitting in the dark.

"Daddy, why are you sitting in Mommy's chair?" I asked him.

"I miss her so much," he said with tears in his eyes.

I wasn't sure I understood. Theirs had been a dysfunctional relationship at best, yet my father seemed unmoored without the woman he had called a malcontent. Now I suspect that the person he missed was the girl he met all those years ago when he was a promising young trumpet player imagining a completely different life for the two of them.

I had never seen my father cry, but he was inconsolable at my mother's funeral. Then God told me something that put it all in perspective: *She was your mother, but she was his girlfriend, lover, wife, confidant and soulmate.*

I wasn't with my father when he died of renal failure in a hospital in Pittsburgh where he wouldn't let anyone see him but Shari. When the doctors suggested dialysis to prolong his life, he asked her to call me.

"Daddy wants to know what you'd do if you were him," she said.

"I wouldn't have dialysis, but I'll respect whatever decision he makes," I told her.

He died two days later. I think my father just needed someone to tell him it was okay to let go. Lately I've been thinking about the model trains he used to build. It was meticulous work that required a lot of patience. Blind in one eye, he'd dip his paintbrush into a pot of color and add a black cat with a white tail in the window of one of the passenger cars. I like to think that I got my attention to detail from him.

In many ways, my parents were polar opposites. Years ago, I gave each of them a credit card "for emergencies." The only caveat was that they call me first if they planned to make a significant purchase so I wouldn't be surprised when I got the bill. One day I got a call from my father, who wanted to know if he could buy one tire for his car. I told him to get four.

My mother, on the other hand, didn't bother to call me before she spent thousands of dollars on evening gowns that I found in her closet years later. None of them had been worn. What I came to understand was that she bought those gowns because they represented the life she had when she and my father dressed up to go out to those swanky supper clubs downtown, a life she believed had been stolen from her.

No one talked about depression in those days, but I suspect that my mother was probably bipolar. One thing I know for sure is that she had a deep well of sadness inside her that no one, not even me or my father, could fill. I wish I could have told my mother that God seeks out and heals the damaged places in each of us.

The key to my salvation has been forgiveness: forgiving those who mistreated or wronged me, forgiving my parents for their shortcomings and forgiving myself for being imperfect.

One of my favorite Bible verses about forgiveness is from Matthew 18: 21, 22: *Then Peter came up and said to him, "Lord, how often shall my brother sin against me, and I forgive him? As many as seven times?" Jesus said to him, "I do not say to you seven times, but seventy times seven."*

For years I created a narrative woven from all of the trauma I had experienced. Now I understand that my life story may not have been as bad as I thought it was. My family wasn't perfect, and we were poor, but I was loved. My parents and my grandmother didn't care if I was gay or straight. They loved me anyway. A lot of my friends weren't that lucky.

The *Course in Miracles* tells us: *I am supported by nature in the process of my self-actualization. As I show up in glory, my life will be glorious. As I celebrate the beauty of life, life will celebrate my beauty. As I relax into the flow of the miraculous, then miracles will find me. I will embody in time the perfection of my true self.*

I have been practicing something I call "praytation" twice a day. It's a combination of prayer and meditation. For the first five minutes, I thank God for everything he's done for me, and I pray for people I love. Then I meditate for ten minutes, emptying my mind of all conscious thought. If God chooses to speak to me, that's when I hear his voice.

What meditation has taught me is to live in the moment instead of contemplating my next move. Worrying about what might happen in the future is useless. Now is all we have. If I had understood that concept years ago, I would have behaved differently. I would have been present.

I used to believe that we are all on this tightrope called life and that there is no net to catch us if we fall. If I was wandering around in the Hamptons or walking along the Hudson River, I'd be overcome with an existential sadness. *What am I doing here? What is my purpose?*

Lately I've come to understand that it's not that complicated. Perhaps we're here simply to make love, make friends, have our hearts broken, watch the sun rise, smell the roses, learn compassion, bestow forgiveness, and experience joy and sadness, love and loss in equal measure. Now when I wonder what I'm doing here, the answer always comes back: You are here just to live.

THE SOUNDTRACK
OF MY LIFE

They Only Come Out at Night by Peter Brown
Does Your Momma Know About Me by The Supremes
Stormy by Classics IV
Stormy by The Supremes
Captain Saint Lucifer by Laura Nyro
Betcha By Golly Wow by Phyllis Hyman
I Love You by Donna Summer
(Theme From) Valley of the Dolls by Dionne Warwick
The Last Ride by Todd Rundgren
Lullaby in Blue by Bette Midler
Where Am I Going? by Dusty Springfield
Knowing When to Leave by Jill O'Hara
Once Upon a Summertime by Barbra Streisand
Didn't We by Barbra Streisand
So Many Stars by Sara Vaughan
Coyote by Joni Mitchell
Who Are You Now? by Barbra Streisand
Cherish by The Association
Who Knows Where the Time Goes by Judy Collins
Moon River by Barbra Streisand
Yes, I'm Ready by Barbara Mason
Spooky by Classics IV
Mercy on Broadway by Laura Nyro
Candidate by David Bowie
Love's About to Change My Heart by Donna Summer

Gonna Get Over You by France Joli
It's Gonna Take a Miracle by The Royalettes
Tears Dry on Their Own by Amy Winehouse
Here's to Life by Shirley Horn
Fireworks by Drake
Trains and Boats and Planes by Dionne Warwick
Endless Love by Diana Ross
The Heart to Break the Heart by France Joli
Flashdance . . . What a Feeling by Irene Cara
You're a Winner by Sharon Redd
Mystery of Love by Donna Summer
Buy and Sell by Laura Nyro
Passionfruit by Drake
Your Heart Belongs to Me by The Supremes
Traces by Classic IV
There Is a Light That Never Goes Out by Morrissey
Simple Kind of Life by Gwen Stefani
Down Deep Inside (Theme From "The Deep") by Donna Summer
Love, Guess Who by Martha and The Vandellas
In My Lonely Room by Martha and The Vandellas
Quicksand by Martha and The Vandellas

ABOUT THE AUTHORS

Brad and I have known each other since 1992 when serendipity brought us together. There's simply no other way to explain what happened. I lived in Los Angeles where I was working for *American Salon*, a trade magazine for beauty professionals, while Brad was the color director at Oribe's salon at Elizabeth Arden in New York City. One day I got a letter from my mother that included a clipping from *The Pittsburgh Press*, the newspaper of record in the town where I grew up.

Brad was famous enough at that point that his hometown newspaper had written a story about him. The first line—*He grew up in a dismal housing project outside of Pittsburgh*—brought me up short. The dismal housing project was Ohio View Acres, which had been built in 1942 as housing for war workers like my father, who was employed by Dravo Corporation on Neville Island where he built LSTs. My family moved out in 1959, the year that Brad's family moved in, so our paths never crossed.

On a whim, I called Oribe's salon. "How dismal was it?" I asked Brad when he came to the phone.

"Who is this?" He sounded suspicious. Later he told me that he never answered the phone while he was working, but something told him to take my call that day. See what I mean? Serendipity.

When I was promoted to publisher and moved to New York two years later, Brad and I forged a friendship, and I became one of his signature buttery blondes. Brad not only wrote a column for *American Salon* called "Dyeing to Know" but he also appeared onstage with me at the International Beauty Show in New York where we talked about the art of hair color for 90 minutes. The audience was captivated.

Brad asked me to write this memoir years ago because I know him better than almost anyone else besides his sister. I couldn't see a way forward at the time since I was still putting out a magazine every month. Two years ago, he asked me again, and this time the stars aligned.

The project tested our friendship at times, especially when he'd clam up if I pressed for details about some painful incident in his past. Brad is a visual person, while I'm a wordsmith so we bickered about everything. I began calling us the "Battling Bickersons," an homage to a popular radio show in the 1940s about a young married couple named John and Blanche Bickerson, who argued about everything much to the delight of their listening audience. At times it felt like pulling teeth to get Brad to provide the details I knew I needed to flesh out his story. I was nearly done writing the first draft when he casually mentioned that he'd met Andy Warhol in 1982 and that his father had played trumpet in backup bands for Billie Holiday and Dizzy Gillespie, information I could have used yesterday! Somehow, we made it to the finish line. As for this book, let's just say that it was a labor of love for both of us.

—*Marianne Dougherty*